Now the serpent was more cunning than any beast of the field which the LORD God had made. And he said to the woman, "Has God indeed said, 'You shall not eat of every tree of the garden'?"

And the woman said to the serpent, "We may eat the fruit of the trees of the garden; but of the fruit of the tree which is in the midst of the garden, God has said, 'You shall not eat it, nor shall you touch it, lest you die.'"

Then the serpent said to the woman, "You will not surely die. For God knows that in the day you eat of it your eyes will be opened, and you will be like God, knowing good and evil."

So when the woman saw that the tree was good for food, that it was pleasant to the eyes, and a tree desirable to make one wise, she took of its fruit and ate. She also gave to her husband with her, and he ate. Then the eyes of both of them were opened, and they knew that they were naked; and they sewed fig leaves together and made themselves coverings.

—Genesis 3:1–7 (NKJV)

Extraordinary Women OF THE BIBLE

HIGHLY FAVORED: MARY'S STORY
SINS AS SCARLET: RAHAB'S STORY
A HARVEST OF GRACE: RUTH AND NAOMI'S STORY
AT HIS FEET: MARY MAGDALENE'S STORY
TENDER MERCIES: ELIZABETH'S STORY
WOMAN OF REDEMPTION: BATHSHEBA'S STORY
JEWEL OF PERSIA: ESTHER'S STORY
A HEART RESTORED: MICHAL'S STORY
BEAUTY'S SURRENDER: SARAH'S STORY
THE WOMAN WARRIOR: DEBORAH'S STORY
THE GOD WHO SEES: HAGAR'S STORY
THE FIRST DAUGHTER: EVE'S STORY

Extraordinary Women OF THE BIBLE

THE FIRST DAUGHTER

EVE'S STORY

Jenelle Hovde

Extraordinary Women of the Bible is a trademark of Guideposts.

Published by Guideposts
100 Reserve Road, Suite E200
Danbury, CT 06810
Guideposts.org

Copyright © 2023 by Guideposts. All rights reserved.

This book, or parts thereof, may not be reproduced, stored in a retrieval system, or transmitted in any form or by any means, electronic, mechanical, photocopying, recording, or otherwise, without the written permission of the publisher.

This is a work of fiction. While the characters and settings are drawn from scripture references and historical accounts, apart from the actual people, events, and locales that figure into the fiction narrative, all other names, characters, places, and events are the creation of the author's imagination or are used fictitiously.

Every attempt has been made to credit the sources of copyrighted material used in this book. If any such acknowledgment has been inadvertently omitted or miscredited, receipt of such information would be appreciated.

Scripture references are from the following sources: The Holy Bible, King James Version (KJV). New American Standard Bible (NASB). Copyright © 1960, 1962, 1963, 1968, 1971, 1972, 1973, 1975, 1977, 1995 by the Lockman Foundation. Used by permission. The Holy Bible, New International Version (NIV). Copyright © 1973, 1978, 1984, 2011 by Biblica, Inc. Used by permission of Zondervan. All rights reserved worldwide. www.zondervan.com. *The Holy Bible, New King James Version (NKJV)*. Copyright © 1982 by Thomas Nelson, Inc. Contemporary English Version (CEV). Copyright © 1991, 1992, 1995 by American Bible Society. Used by permission.

Cover and interior design by Müllerhaus
Cover illustration by Brian Call represented by Illustration Online LLC.
Typeset by Aptara, Inc.

ISBN 978-1-961126-06-0 (hardcover)
ISBN 978-1-961126-07-7 (epub)

Printed and bound in the United States of America
10 9 8 7 6 5 4 3 2 1

Extraordinary Women OF THE BIBLE

THE FIRST DAUGHTER

EVE'S STORY

DEDICATION

For my sweet daughters. I love you.
You are such a wonderful gift from God.
I can't wait to see what He does in your lives.

ACKNOWLEDGMENTS

I'd like to thank my wonderful editors at Guideposts, Sabrina Diaz, Jane Haertel, and Ellen Tarver. Their wisdom and encouragement have helped me craft each novel. I'd also like to thank my agent, Tamela Hancock Murray, who has blessed me with her enthusiasm and dedication.

I'd also like to recognize my fabulous critique partners, Maddie Morrow, Shannon McNear, Jayna Breigh, Rachelle Gonzalez, and Jason. Thank you for your insight and friendship. You bless me more than I can say! Thank you to M., my archeologist friend in Israel. You are amazing!

To my husband and daughters, thank you again for being so patient as I spent hours dreaming, planning, and writing. I couldn't do this without you. Thank you for your support. I love you!

I'd like to thank my church family for the constant encouragement and prayers. I certainly felt those prayers during the late midnight hours while writing.

I'd love to recognize my grandmother and my mother, who gifted me with stories about Jesus. I can only pray I pass on your legacy to my daughters. What a gift to grow in a home where God came first! I am forever grateful for both of you.

Finally, I'd like to thank God for His wonderful mercy and forgiveness. Biblical fiction is a joy to write, but it can never supplant God's Word. My prayer and hope is that readers will be encouraged to dive into the Bible and study it for themselves.

Cast of CHARACTERS

Abel • the second son of Adam and Eve
Adam • the first man
Alon • the son of Calah and Abel
Ariel • a daughter of Eve
Cain • the eldest son of Adam and Eve
Calah • a twin daughter of Adam and Eve
cherubim • angels created by God
Edina • a twin daughter of Adam and Eve
Enoch • the son of Cain and Edina
Eve • the first woman
Father • Eve's term for God, who created her
The serpent • the tempter of Eve and Adam

CHAPTER ONE

Awaken. The voice, deep yet melodious, whispered within her, stirring her to obey.

Awaken, My daughter. He sounded almost...amused. She blinked. Once. Twice. Several things threaded through her as warmth surged into her limbs, forcing them to twitch and finally move.

Whoever owned that voice deeply loved her, and she wanted to meet Him. Somehow, she knew He differed from her. If the warmth of life rippled through her, so did ideas, thoughts, and visions, each drop of knowledge a gift from the One who created her. Her eyelids fluttered again, her vision honing and sharpening until she stared into a bright expanse overhead.

"Here is flesh like my flesh. Is she...alive?" Another voice, one much younger, his timbre trembling with excitement.

"Oh yes. I suspect you'll have much to show her." Again, the older voice.

She inhaled another deep breath, this time noting the distinct scents. More sensations flooded through her as she lay on her back. She heard something chirping behind her, and tiny things rustling in the grass beside her head. The surface she rested on felt damp and cool. She shifted ever so slightly, her mind telling her body what to do, and her limbs obeyed.

"How soon?" the younger voice asked.

"Very soon, My son."

"Can she understand us, Father?"

"Yes. I've planted My words in her. As for the rest, I'll let you teach her."

With a burst of energy, she sat up from the ground as curiosity about both voices pulled at her. Long grass stirred beside her, tickling her arms and back. It was soft. And it smelled good.

Searching for the voice that bid her to awaken, she scanned her surroundings—a vibrant world unfolding before her. There was so much to see, to take in, and to study. Yet the sights in front of her were not enough to compete with that loving Presence who commanded her to live. "Father, where are You?"

A gentle wind brushed her hair and cheek as she searched for the One who made her, but He was not in the wind, nor in the grass, nor in the sky above her.

Even so, she heard His voice all the same. *I am here, My child. You speak correctly. I am your Maker, your Father. But unlike your flesh, I am Spirit. I see all things, and I am everywhere.*

Around her, trees and palms of vibrant green shook their foliage in deference as the breeze gathered strength. Somehow, she knew Father was next to her. She felt His pride and pleasure in His creation. His uncontainable joy. And she was His very own. His beloved daughter.

She glanced down at her body, her dusky skin glistening beneath the sunlight. Long legs made to jump and run. Arms to...

"She is beautiful," the younger voice breathed. Awe softened his tone. "So very beautiful."

Then she saw the owner of the eager youthful voice. He lay almost hidden in the long grass, his hands brushing absently against his chest as he stared at her.

"Who are you?" she blurted.

A smile softened his angular features as he pushed up from the ground. "I am called Adam." He rose to his full height, his legs more defined and muscular than hers. And her breath caught when he knelt in front of her. Black hair played about his forehead and curled around his neck. And his eyes. They glowed—the same bright color as the grass beneath her body. He captured her chin with his hand, gently turning her face from one side to the other.

"Very beautiful," he said again, clearly pleased. "I think I shall call you woman. Made from my flesh, indeed. For that is what woman means. 'Out of man.'"

The grip of his fingers softened as he traced a line down her cheek. "And I have seen much of the beauty that Father has made, from the meadow filled with white flowers to the south of us, to the tawny lioness who feeds her cub. Even the Tree of Life."

She shivered, partly from the heat emanating from his lithe form and the way he studied her. His smile widened at her reaction. To her surprise, he reached for her and pulled her up onto unsteady legs. She swayed once and felt his arms immediately band about her, firm and secure. His gaze dropped to her lips, and his embrace tightened.

Something sparked inside of her. Something...*beautiful*, to echo Adam.

"Father, may I show her the garden?" Adam asked, yet he couldn't tear his gaze from her.

Yes.

The answer resonated deep within her. She saw no physical form of God, but she felt His presence just as strongly as Adam's.

"I don't want to leave You, Father," she said as longing filled her to know more of her Creator.

Tomorrow, I will meet again with you, Beloved Daughter. How marvelous. She could hear Him inside her thoughts.

Without warning, Adam swooped one muscular arm beneath her legs and the other around her waist. Pressed against his hard chest, she watched the world around her as he strode down the hill toward a vast meadow of flowers, describing what he could to her. White delicate petals fluttered, matching the hue of white clouds floating in the blue sky.

"Why have I been made?" she asked.

His eyes remained on her as he moved quickly, sure-footed of the path winding before him.

"For our Father's pleasure"—his voice grew husky—"and because He thought it wasn't good that I would be without a partner."

She grinned at him and was rewarded with the sensation of his chest pounding all the harder. "Then, Adam, you will never be alone again."

His green eyes flared, and his arms tightened around her. "Father meets with me every day and walks in the garden. Everything you see, He created. He watches over every living creature. We are blessed with His companionship. No one is ever truly alone in Eden."

There was so much to take in as she studied her new world. The forest to the right of her, lush with trailing vines and rustling trees, beckoned her to dive into the cool depths. Inside the foliage, creatures frolicked, darting among the wide leaves, hiding among the dappled shadows and wavering sunlight. To the front of her, a vista spread out in every direction with a dark blue line cutting through it.

"There is the river." Adam nodded toward the blue line, as if reading her thoughts. "From there, if we follow the riverbank, we will find the most luscious fruit groves, full of the juiciest peaches, plums, and mangos you ever tasted, and then I'll show you the vegetables and the—"

Her stomach grumbled in response.

His gaze snagged on hers, and they both giggled at the same time. He smelled wonderful—like the grass she had lain upon and other delicious scents too.

"Maybe we should eat first before exploring," he said as he carried her. He halted beneath a tree loaded with dangling green globes.

"Avocados," he explained as he set her on her feet. After plucking one, he handed it to her. "Taste it. You won't be disappointed."

Following his example, she peeled back the smooth, dark green skin and bit into the fragrant green flesh. The avocado burst with flavor, bits of it melting on her fingertips. She ate the entire thing right down to the hard core and licked her fingers while Adam stared at her.

"I knew you'd enjoy it," he murmured before finishing his fruit.

She did. In response, her body felt a quickening of energy and strength while the hunger abated.

"Everywhere you look, you'll find food. But I think the mangoes might be my favorite treats, second to the avocado. Whenever I'm thirsty, I drink from the river. I'll show you how when you are ready."

"Ready for what?" she asked as she examined the enormous round seed remaining on her palm.

"To walk." He bumped her shoulder with a teasing glint in his eyes. "Unless you would like me to carry you? Because I rather like holding you."

She liked the feel of him too. She took a step and then another, stopping only to toss the seed. Her legs worked perfectly. Her arms as well. So, perhaps he hadn't needed to carry her after all. But before she could answer further, he spun on his heel and ran away from her, his legs pumping.

He paused only long enough to throw over his shoulder, "Come on, sleepyhead. I can't promise I'll leave too many mangoes for you."

Could she run the way he did? Part of her wanted to stand still and enjoy the magnificent sight before her, of the man running at full speed, and part of her wanted to join Adam.

Go, her Father quietly urged. *You are strong enough to run.*

With a hoot of joy, she sprang forward, the muscles in her legs contracting and strengthening. At first, she lurched forward, her feet stumbling in the spongy dirt, and then she picked up speed, her feet and legs moving faster and faster as the wind tugged at her hair.

Animals stopped to stare. So many kinds, she could scarcely take it all in as she darted past them. Above, strange creatures flapped wings and soared high then dipped low to race beside her. Almost as fast as that wind surging with her, she swept over the meadow, gathering in speed and strength, only to merge with a herd of animals who perked at her arrival. With one accord, they galloped on either side, kicking up clumps of dirt behind their hooves.

Deer. Her Father breathed the word into her mind. *See how fleet-footed I have made them? As wonderful as they are, they do not compare to you, My Daughter.*

Adam stopped at the rise of yet another small hill dotted with wildflowers. Now it was his turn to study her. His grin widened as if he couldn't quite believe what he saw. Laughter bubbled up inside her as she rushed to join him. Such joy. Such freedom.

The deer thundered past, the herd dividing to avoid hitting Adam, although one creature halted long enough to nudge a wet nose against his hand.

She felt the whoosh of air as the animals rushed past her. "Our Father told me these are deer."

Adam nodded. "I know. I named them. He tasked me with naming all the creatures."

She inhaled again, her heart thudding inside her chest. Her fingers trembled and her legs quivered with excitement, but she wanted nothing more than to race again and push herself to the limit.

But Adam reached yet again for her hand, his long fingers curling around hers. "Come. I have so much to show you. So much to tell you."

At the river's edge, he pointed out flashing bodies darting beneath the clear water. Fish, with sheer fins fluttering in the current, swarmed him when he dipped his hand into the sparkling water. He cupped those sculpted fingers, showing her how to drink. Mesmerized by the shape of his collarbone and the strong lines of his throat and jaw, she tore her attention from him and focused on the river. Whenever she gazed upon him, the rhythm beating inside her only managed to increase. She reached into the water, where bright blue and red fish swam into her hands as if wishing for her touch. She hadn't realized she was thirsty, and the water eased down her throat.

Adam shared names of the various animals as she drank. A tawny lion rubbed against the legs of a stout elephant that stopped to brush its trunk against the lion's back. She could hear the purr of the mighty feline from where she sat, and it brought a smile to her face. The sound echoed the happiness mounting within her.

Everything was so marvelous. So exciting. So new.

An eagle soared past her, with mighty wings outstretched in flight as it caught a breeze. Perhaps best of all, a delicate butterfly alighted on her shoulder, flexing pale yellow wings flecked with orange. So many names. Yet somehow she remembered each one that Adam informed her of. Everywhere she looked, a new delight awaited her. A bright ball of fire shone in the sky. Adam called it the sun. A faint moon hovered above her, a pale circle opposite of the sun, yet no less stunning.

"How did Father make all of this?" she asked Adam.

He leaned back on his haunches, pulling his hand out of the river. A few fish jumped out of the water, spraying crystal drops, as if to coax him to play again.

"Father spoke everything you see into existence. First, He separated the waters, making the heavens. Then He made the land and seas appear and then the grass and the flowers. He placed the stars and planets above us. Tonight, you'll see those very planets sparkle in a black sky. He made the fish in the seas and birds that fly in the sky. He made the animals, and He made me. And now you."

"Did He speak me into existence? Why don't we look like the other animals?"

"You are special." Adam pulled a clump of grass, allowing the dirt to shake free from the delicate roots. "He sculpted me from the dust, and He formed you from one of my ribs. We were made to reflect His image and His glory. We are different from the animals. It is our privilege to watch over the garden and take care of the land and all the creatures. Of all the beasts here, we alone have the gift of communing with Him."

She reached out for the dirt and squished it between her fingers. It was moist and crumbly. A spicy fragrance immediately filled her nostrils. She lowered her head to sniff her hands again. Such an entrancing scent, different from the grass, the flowers, and the earth itself. A melody of fragrance waited to entice her whenever or wherever she sniffed.

When she raised her head, Adam laughed. He reached out and brushed the crumbs of dirt from her nose. "It is a wonderful life. But it's better now that you are here. I didn't realize how much I wanted—no, *needed*—a partner until I saw you lying on the grass. Father knows exactly what we need, and He provides it."

Her day merged into a blur of events. She traced with her finger the thin lines of shiny yellow and white metal scaling massive rocks. Gold, Adam called it. Crystals encrusted other boulders, catching the rays of the sun and fragmenting it into many-colored lights. The earth, the rocks, the trees, the flowers, the animals... It was all a declaration of Father's creativity and joy. Above, the sky blazed in vibrant hues of blue.

She found the other orchards of fruit and tasted a fragrant mango. Juice dripped down her chin as she savored the pulpy yellow flesh. Later, she plucked a handful of wildflowers and placed a few in her hair. Even Adam helped her, his face once again wreathed in a grin. Everywhere she went, animals approached Adam as if eager for his affection. His touch.

By the time the sun moved west, they sank onto another hill next to the river, watching it vanish into the horizon. To her delight, Adam wrapped his arm around her waist.

He smiled at her. "When I was tasked with naming the creatures, there were none who could match me. None who could truly speak with me. For many days, I sat on this hill at sunset and watched the animals pairing off. Now, I've been given you. I could not ask for a better gift."

Exhilaration spread in her chest at his admission. Wonderful exhilaration to be with such a partner, and she wished the day would never end. She rested her head against his solid shoulder, watching as the sky changed from a brilliant red to a muted pink, and then deep purple. One by one, glittering lights appeared in the sky, heralding her first night. Adam pointed out a red planet, and then the glimmering North Star. The sky was a marvel, reflecting worlds far beyond her own.

She had discovered so much.

"What else is left to explore?" she asked. Would he show her beyond the river, to the vast horizon in the distance? Or would he show her more animals? "Can we leave the garden and discover what lies beyond?"

He shoved his hand through his tousled hair, his brow pinched even if his lips quirked with amusement. "Why would we want to leave paradise? Eden has everything we need."

She nodded slowly. Adam's answer made sense, but her gaze wandered to the faint horizon where the river broke into four tributaries, emptying into the unknown. From the vantage point of the hill, she realized Eden was mostly enclosed by a rock wall, the sole opening where the river drained. She could see almost everything in the garden from the hill. The meadow where the animals frolicked lay to the East. To the west, orchards blossomed with fruit. A densely forested area hid the central part of the garden—the last place left for her to discover.

"There are many special things in Eden. Tomorrow, I will show you the trees," Adam murmured in her ear, earning another shiver rippling through her.

"Trees?" she asked, thinking of the palms and cedars and fruit trees Adam had insisted she see. Perhaps she would discover more secrets tucked inside the magnificent garden.

"Two trees." The playfulness in his tone diminished. He said no more, instead distracting her with his touch, as he ran his fingers lightly across her shoulders and then her back. Night had fallen, and the song of crickets filled the silence, along with the subtle wind rushing through the foliage. The moon rose high and bright, flooding the landscape with a cool light. And as she lay down beside him, more questions flooded her mind.

"Why are they special? Do they have fruit?"

"One of them is forbidden. We may not eat of it."

She tasted the strange word. Forbidden? What did that mean, exactly? "But why is it forbidden? Why can't I eat from it?"

Adam rolled over to face her. "You'll have to ask Father in the morning. But now it is time to sleep."

Sleep? She was about to protest when he pressed a finger against her lips. Then he stretched out his long frame and yawned. She snuggled into him, feeling the rise and fall of his muscled chest. A rumble came deep in his throat as he played with a stray lock of her black hair.

"Thank You, Father," she whispered as sleepiness washed over her.

A swift answer rode on the edge of the warm wind. *I love you, Daughter. I love you so much.*

Surrounded by that very love, she let herself drift to a place of dreams.

What could possibly surpass such a perfect day?

CHAPTER TWO

She woke before Adam. What a delight to watch him sleep, with a muscular arm flung behind his head and his hair falling over his brow—enticing enough for her to brush that stray lock aside. How different he was when compared to her. Yet, for all their differences, how similar they were. Fitting to each other as perfectly as could be. And he thought her beautiful. The memory of his words brought a pleasant heat to her cheeks. She scooted forward in the grass, unwilling to awaken him just yet.

The ground had proven comfortable and refreshing, cushioning her every movement. She dreamed last night of stars and planets, and elephants and lions. Wrapping her arms about her knees, she watched pink dawn brighten the land. Adam had shared more names of colors. Some things she knew instinctively, others her Father or Adam explained whenever she asked.

Today, she would meet again with her Father. Longing flared within her, to speak with Him and learn more. She would see the two trees Adam had mentioned. When would Father make His appearance? Already she missed Him.

A glint of light flashed on the horizon, next to the rock barrier surrounding the garden. She leaped from the ground and shielded her eyes. The brilliant sun rose, flooding the plain and her hill while obscuring the point of light. Was the flashing light her Father?

It flickered again, zooming through a puff of clouds until it disappeared. A rustle at her side indicated Adam was awake. He followed her line of sight.

"I saw a light in the clouds. It did not stay put, unlike the stars we saw last night."

Adam stared at the clouds for a moment. "There are others. Angels. They serve our Father in the heavenly realm, watching over our garden. They don't speak to me. But sometimes I've seen them in the early dawn. They will probably leave us alone."

"Are they like us?"

Adam shook his head. "No. Not exactly. They are also in a spirit form, like Father. I see them only as a glimmer or a shadow, and rarely at that."

Her skin prickled with awareness, signaling something altogether powerful and too wonderful for words, a presence so majestic she felt foolish for assuming that a mere dot of light could be Him.

She whirled around and cried out with joy, "Father!"

"Did you enjoy what I have made, little one?" that beloved deep voice asked.

Although she didn't see her Father, she felt His presence as surely as Adam's, who stood beside her.

"Very much," she enthused. "Adam says he will show me the two trees."

Adam bowed his head. "I waited for You to tell her everything."

When Father spoke, the flowers quivered at her feet, and a sense of awe suffused her at His majesty and power. "Walk with Me, children. I will take you to the trees and explain what you need to know."

She learned on her walk that the garden was called Eden, the place of pleasure. She rather liked the new word.

To her delight, Father proved Himself to have a wonderful sense of humor as He called other creatures to Adam. Some beasts appeared stately with long necks and legs, while others, like the round pink pig rolling in the silt near the riverbank, made her chuckle. She watched an adorable bird fly up to her with bright red wings and a hooked beak. It mimicked what she said, squawking loudly. Giggling, she told the bird to say hello, and it did, over and over, while bobbing its crimson head.

Even her Father laughed.

"Can the animals speak?" she asked Him.

"I have created you and Adam with language," Father explained. "This bird can only mimic what you say. It has no true understanding, unlike you. You've been given something precious—a soul that communes with me."

The wind nudged her to keep walking. She waved goodbye to the brilliant red and gold bird and followed Adam past an orchard into another meadow dotted with orange and yellow flowers. The river, which she had seen previously, quietly gurgled near the trees.

She had no eyes for the gorgeous flowers. Instead, she gasped when she saw both of the trees.

One stood tall with a white trunk spotted with gray whorls. Its delicate leaves sparkled gold in the sun. The second was squat and lower in height, with a gnarled trunk digging thick roots into the soil. It was no less striking, with broad blue-tinted leaves and heavy purple fruit dangling from the stout branches.

But there was something unusual about it.

An air of heaviness, perhaps. Or was it a shadow, as if the tree had a cloud above it, obscuring its full glory? The Tree of Life, however, glowed beneath the sunlight, with its branches outstretched in welcome.

Adam's smile diminished as he halted midstep beside her. He did not approach the bluish tree. When she moved forward to examine the heavy fruit, he reached out and snagged her arm. "Wait."

A breeze rustled the leaves of both trees. She sensed Father near her.

"Be fruitful and multiply; fill the earth and subdue it; have dominion over the fish of the sea, over the birds of the air, and over every living thing that moves on the earth. See, I have given you every herb that yields seed which is on the face of all the earth, and every tree whose fruit yields seed; to you it shall be for food. Also, to every beast of the earth, to every bird of the air, and to everything that creeps on the earth, in which there is life, I have given every green herb for food."

"Here is your choice, Daughter. Before you is the golden tree, the Tree of Life. You may eat of its leaves and live forever, including your children. The other tree is the Tree of Knowledge of Good and Evil. I have given you both nearly everything to eat and savor in Eden. But you must not eat from this one tree. If you do, you will surely die."

Death.

She glanced at Adam, who had paled.

Questions bubbled up within her, but she nodded in agreement. She knew enough, didn't she? She didn't dare ask for more. After all, the power emanating from her Father pressed slivers of warning into her mind. As He explained her role in Eden, to be a helpmate to Adam, and to tend to the garden, the plants, and the animals, she did her best to listen, but her thoughts kept drifting back to the heavy, mysterious tree that seemed to call to her spirit.

The forbidden tree.

The garden of Eden proved to be immense. In the days that followed, it had been more than enough to follow Adam and learn everything she could. She did not return to the Tree of Knowledge of Good and Evil. The Tree of Life was only to be used periodically, offering healing when needed—a mere nibble of a leaf, bringing rejuvenation.

She avoided the center of the garden, focusing more and more on the perimeters, where she discovered the wonder of seeds, some floating on the breeze with tufts gyrating outward and others transported via the beaks of birds.

But that didn't mean her mind didn't stray to the image of purple fruit so dark they reminded her of the night. What types of seeds resided in that fruit? Did it even have seeds? With a sigh, she thrust aside the thoughts as she tended to a cluster of plants pushing through the soil beside an array of crimson flowers. As she moved the moist dirt to help the fragile buds emerge sooner, a tiny green bird landed on her shoulder, the wings beating so fast that she felt a welcome breeze again on her cheek. How small it was. She reached out a finger, allowing it a perch. Gently, she lowered the bird into the nearest red flower to drink nectar.

The animals granted her the same affectionate access as they did Adam, but it was the flowers and the trees that called to her. Father told her that she could help steer the plants as she so desired, seeding different areas. He taught her how to prune the vines and branches—a simple task but an enjoyable one as she pulled and shaped the rough bark or the tender buds.

Moments earlier, she had discovered a new variety of long grass with kernels bursting from a head. When she pinched off the kernel and nibbled it, a sweet-nutty flavor hit her tongue. Could she encourage more of the long grass to grow? She couldn't wait to show Adam something new for a change. Something he didn't already know.

Laughter filled the valley, distracting her from her task. Pivoting, she saw Adam cradling a little lamb in his arms as he jogged toward her.

"Come!" he shouted when he saw her. "A ewe had babies! *Babies!*"

She leaped from the ground, leaving behind the red flowers and the tiny bird sipping its fill. Wonder filled her at the idea of a newborn. Hadn't she watched several of the sheep mate? At last, she would see marvel of birth. Adam reached her with a long-legged stride. From the cocoon of his arms, a small white form bleated.

"Isn't she adorable?" He crooned to the lamb with a tender expression on his face. "I won't keep you much longer from your mother, little one."

The walk wasn't far to the mother ewe. To her delight, the sheep lay next to a massive tawny lion, who kept shade over the new mother. Another lamb lay asleep, curled next to his mother while other animals munched quietly on the grass.

The sight of a lamb in Adam's arms did an odd thing to her chest. An overpowering urge filled her to nestle it.

"May I have a turn?" she asked, already holding out her hands to take hold of the newborn.

Adam gently placed the trembling lamb in her arms. It felt warm and fluffy and smelled of grass and earth. A tiny chest beat against her hands, and she pressed it closer to her skin.

Closing her eyes, she savored the moment. When she blinked, she caught Adam staring at her with the sweetest of expressions.

"I can hardly wait to see you embrace a child of our own one day." His voice dipped to a husky level. "You'll be a wonderful mother."

She could hardly wait either. Carefully, she lowered the lamb next to its mother to nurse and stepped back, chuckling when the nearby lion yawned before closing its eyes to sleep.

When she straightened, she bumped into Adam. Before she could move out of the way, he dipped his head and pressed his lips against hers.

When he pulled away, she touched her mouth. "What was that?"

His mouth quirked to the side. "I think I shall call *that* a kiss."

"Do it again," she breathed.

And to her complete joy, he obeyed.

Evening fell, bringing new colors to the sky. This time, from the vantage spot on top of the hill that allowed the best view of Eden, she observed a sunset of muted purples and brilliant pinks. The purple reminded her of the mysterious Tree of Knowledge of Good and Evil. A shuffling sound drew her attention away from the sunset. Adam flung himself on the ground, his arm behind his neck.

They had experienced a full day watching over other ewes who delivered babies with barely a sound. Soon the meadow would be filled with frolicking lambs.

"I think one lioness will have cubs soon," Adam remarked. He had grabbed a cluster of grapes on the return walk to their hill where they rested. He kept his hand outstretched, ready to share them with her. She shook her head. These grapes, one of many varieties in Eden, appeared almost black in the gathering dusk.

"Adam, why does God forbid us the Tree of Knowledge of Good and Evil?"

He shrugged before dangling a fat globe into his mouth before chewing.

"Surely there is a reason. Why put it there in the middle of Eden and tell us not to eat it? Why must we die if we eat its fruit?"

Adam swallowed the last of his grapes and tossed aside the stem. "I don't really know why Father asks us to leave it alone. He makes decisions I can't always fully understand. I just know He chooses what is good."

All around her, further evidence of goodness of God waited to be discovered. Adam was right of course. But the idea of a choice intrigued her. She couldn't stop thinking about that choice and what it really meant.

"Besides, why do you care about the fruit of one tree?" Adam tapped her knee with a finger. "I watched you eat your share of oranges and peppers. I think you ate only the orange colors today."

A light laugh escaped her. "Not true. I had a purple carrot earlier."

She had been with Adam long enough to know when he teased her. Nudging his shoulder with hers, she explained further. "It's not just about the fruit. It's about the knowledge. Father knows so much about, well, everything. I want to know too. I want to know why the birds can fly above us, but we can't fly with them. I want to know where the sun flees when it dips into the earth. I want to know more about the beings of light you and I've seen. I want to know how to make flowers of my own and—"

"You will learn much in the days to come." Adam sat up from his reclined position and reached for her. "Father knows best, and when He wants to reveal something new, He will."

She leaned against her partner and stared at the twilight descending over the land. One by one, stars flared to life, pointing to constellations and marvelous worlds far, far beyond her own. What would it be like to have so much power to create the universe and everything in it with just a few words? Who indeed, could be as awe-inspiring and as powerful as her Father? Who could surpass such wisdom and majesty?

A firm arm wrapped around her middle as Adam whispered into her ear, his breath fanning her skin. "We have so much to enjoy, don't we? So much more than just one tree."

She settled into his embrace, noting how his chest beat all the harder the closer she came to him. If there was one new thing she had learned, Adam needed to be touched.

"Perhaps we could kiss again," he murmured into her hair as his fingers skimmed her arms, tracing an indiscernible pattern that made her heart match rhythm.

"Perhaps," she agreed with a small grin.

"Oh Woman," he murmured as he brushed his lips against her shoulder. "Have I told you lately how beautiful you are? How much I love you? Desire you?"

He had. Many times.

Of all the things she had discovered in the garden, Adam remained the best and brightest of gifts. Judging from the way he breathed further endearments into her ear or cupped her face to kiss her deeply, she knew he felt the same. In these precious moments, love shone as radiant as moon above, filling her with great joy. How satisfying to have someone to hold, to delight in, to cherish forever.

By the time the moon and stars shifted in the sky and Adam was fast asleep, she stood and moved to the edge of the hill, so not to awaken him. The dim light highlighted the garden with touches of silver. She could see the gleaming river, leading to the Tree of Knowledge of Good and Evil. A copse of cedar trees hid it from her view, but the image of it had been imprinted in her mind.

The forbidden tree was not hers to do with as she pleased. But, as Adam had noted, she had so much to discover and enjoy. Pressing her hands against her heated cheeks, she smiled again as she thought of Adam and the pleasant moments spent upon their hill.

A contented sigh escaped her as she headed back to her sleeping spot next to him. As she ducked beneath one outstretched branch, a subdued rattle stopped her. She brushed aside the foliage, arrested when two silver eyes flickered at her with irises constricting to narrow slits. With a sinuous grace, the serpent flexed glittering scales and glided along the tree branch. Instead of approaching her the way the other animals did, it entwined its body onto another branch and pattered away on short legs. She pushed farther into the branches, grasping for it. A white forked tongue flickered in and out between its stiff lips. And then it disappeared into the shadows.

"Wait, come back," she whispered. Was it her imagination that the serpent halted at her command?

She had seen nothing quite like it. Should she wake Adam up and insist he see the serpent too? But Adam's deep breathing suggested he was fast asleep, and a quick glance at the tree revealed nothing but darkness, until a gleam of pearlescent scales undulated behind the leaves.

Was it her imagination, or did someone call her name? Something unfamiliar but, oh, that voice…it was like liquid moonlight.

Woman.

CHAPTER THREE

At dawn, she felt Adam trace her cheek and promise to return soon with breakfast after he checked on the lambs. Instead of rising with him, she rolled over on her spot, far too comfortable to leave, her eyelids fluttering shut again with drowsiness before a rattle echoed near her head.

Opening one eye, she found herself face-to-face with the magnificent serpent. Gilded with the impending sunrise, it was far more glorious than she remembered. Far larger too, with a body half the length as hers. It cocked its flat head, the frill around it as delicate as a flower or a dragonfly wing.

"You finally came to say hello," she muttered as she reached out to caress it. "I wonder what Adam calls you?"

It nudged her hand, brushing against it like the lion cubs did, but unlike the wool of lambs and the fur of the cubs, the serpent's scales felt cold and slippery against her palm.

"He has no name for me," the serpent spoke, his white tongue flickering in and out between its lips. "But what should I call you, First Daughter?"

She shot up from the ground, snatching her hand to her breast. "Wait—you-you speak?"

The serpent chuckled, his eyes contracting and widening as he swayed upward, his unfolding in a display similar to the blue peacocks.

The laugh was so charming and the serpent so lovely, she forgot her initial shock and reached out to him again. With another rattle, almost as if he was pleased, he encircled her arm, sliding around it, inching closer. "I speak. Quite well, in fact."

"I saw a red bird that tried to mimic me."

The coiled body squeezed slightly around her arm. "I am not a parrot. And you have yet to tell me your name."

"Woman," she answered as she reached out to stroke his head. Hadn't he already called out her name the night before?

"Woman," he said slowly as if tasting the word. "Woman. It means drawn out of man, doesn't it? Yes, I believe you were taken from Adam's rib, and made second. Hmm. I wonder why God didn't make *you* first? Why don't you pick a better name? Try again, First Daughter. Surely you can dream up something with far more imagination."

She had no answer for his musings. Indeed, he only confused her with such strange talk. So, instead, she quickly changed the subject. "How is it that you talk and none of the others do?"

"Ah, of course you would ask. You're quite the curious one, aren't you? I've watched you for days now, digging into the meadow and sniffing the roots."

"There's so much to learn—"

"Yes." The serpent released his grip on her and dangled until she lowered him to the ground. "Yes, there is. Have you discovered everything yet?"

She rubbed her arms, prickles flaring across them. "Not the Tree of Knowledge of Good and Evil. That one is forbidden to us."

It reared up a second time, the frill flaring outward. "Did God really say, 'You must not eat from any tree in the garden?'"

She frowned at the question. "We may eat fruit from the trees in the garden but God did say, 'You must not eat fruit from the tree that is in the middle of the garden, and you must not touch it, or you will die.'"

"You will certainly not die." The serpent's tone sharpened with derision and the heavy air around her cooled until she felt chilled enough to wrap her arms about her middle. "For God knows that when you eat from it, your eyes will be opened, and you will be like God, knowing good and evil."

Oh? Her hands fluttered near her chest as she mulled over its words. Why would God do such a thing, keeping the very best from her? It didn't make sense, not considering all she knew of her Father. But then again, why did He test her so?

"Did you eat from it?" she finally dared to ask.

The irises of those magnificent eyes widened, the blackness nearly swallowing the eyes entirely. "What do you think, little one? After all, am I not one of many serpents in Eden? Now look at me. Imagine how you will change if you have the courage to take a bite. True freedom awaits if you do. Imagine the possibilities if you could determine your own path."

"I can choose what I do," she protested, rubbing her arms even more furiously.

The serpent crept up the outstretched tree overhanging her hill until he was at eye level and could meet her gaze. "Tending the garden and having children? Never leaving the garden perimeter? Haven't you seen the world beyond Eden? Forgive me, but your choices seem to be limited to being a servant to your Adam as you live out the rest of your days doing as he tells you."

She swallowed hard, her throat suddenly dry. It was true that she had never left the garden. And yes, she had wondered what awaited beyond the borders of Eden. Nor had she really questioned her role as a helpmate to Adam before. She wasn't even sure what being a servant meant. Adam had already brought her so much joy, sharing everything he had with her. And she with him. But now, to hear the serpent describe her current life with so much curdling disdain…

Had her Father—God—lied to her? Had God kept the power completely for Himself, relegating her to a lesser, weaker role? If the serpent ate of the fruit and still lived, and evolved into something remarkable, perhaps she might change as well?

"It's forbidden," she repeated as she stepped backward.

A fierce light entered the serpent's eyes. "Nothing is ever truly forbidden unless you decide it so, Woman. *Nothing*. But you're clever, and one day, I think you'll have the courage to find the strength within you to truly break free and discover all the wonder that is hiding inside of you. You just need to see your worth, your true worth."

Her hair bounced as she shook her head. "No, no—"

The serpent bowed to her, suddenly deferential, though he dug his claws into the bark of the branch, leaving gouges in his wake. Yet his voice remained melodious. "Forgive me. I forget that so few have had my courage. I alone have tasted from the tree. But be at peace, Daughter. It's a challenge not for the faint at heart. I've placed too much too soon on you. Go back to birthing your lambs and digging in the dirt. You'll be happier there in the end. And a word to the wise—tell no one of our conversation. Not everyone was meant to be a god."

His words arrested her, pinning her to the spot. Was *godhood* what she was missing out on by avoiding the tree? Would she change into something far more lovely, more wise, and all-knowing if she tasted its fruit?

But before she could ask another question, the serpent winked at her and disappeared into the tree.

CHAPTER FOUR

She did not see the serpent for several days—not in the tree above her hill, nor in the meadow filled with flowers.

Her lips flattened every time she felt the urge to talk with Adam, or her Father. But she thought about the creature and his words, flipping them over and over in her mind.

"Not everyone was meant to be a god."

Several days and nights had passed in the garden when Adam declared a day of rest one morning.

"Father made the heavens and the earth, including everything you see. But on the seventh day, He rested. We get to rest as well."

"I don't need any more sleep." She laughed as she rolled over on the ground, missing his arm when he swung out to tug a lock of her hair. "Why does God sleep on the seventh day?"

"Rest. Not sleep. I think He does it more to set an example for us. It's not as though He truly needs to rest. We do, however. The same way we need sleep, food, and water. You haven't swum in the lake yet, have you? The turtles will carry you on their backs, if you do."

Thoroughly curious, she traipsed after him, pausing only to snag an apple to eat on her morning walk. The serpent was far from her mind by the time she stood at the bank of the lake where a fringe of reeds swayed with each changing direction of the wind. Giant lily pads with massive blossoms slowly twirled as turtles swam past.

With a hoot, Adam ran and flung himself into the water with a great splash, submerging completely. When he bobbed up out of the water, gasping for air, she hesitated. He raised his hand, beckoning for her to follow.

She did but not with a splash as big as his. The water remained so clear, she could see the silty bottom, including the turtles that swam past her, some nibbling on the billowing algae. The green turtles were large, half her height, and very gentle, moving slowly on land but surprisingly quick in the water.

Adam allowed one to pull him on a ride toward the bottom of the lake where the algae danced in the waves. She nearly giggled at the sight as bubbles floated past, streaming from his mouth and nostrils. Then she felt a nudge as one turtle bumped against her leg, offering the same ride. Gulping a deep breath into her lungs, she held on to the bumpy shell and allowed the turtle to submerge and descend. A new world waited below the surface. A few fish with iridescent scales darted above her, shaded by the enormous round lily pads. Adam swung around, still holding on to his turtle. When he released its shell, he kicked his legs and moved his arms, swimming like a fish. With exaggerated gestures, he showed her how to paddle until she could no longer hold air.

Motioning her need to breathe, she kicked her legs and headed upward, following the stream of sunlight wavering in the current. He easily caught up to her and pulled her along as they broke the surface, both gasping for air.

"How wonderful!" she exclaimed as water dripped down her nose.

He treaded water with one arm, still holding her. "You'll learn to swim in no time. The water in this lake is fairly shallow. It's the seas outside our garden that stretch as far and as deep as the eye can see."

She tried to tread water as he did. "That much water? Have you seen it?"

He offered a wry grin. "Father told me how He made the waters and the massive sea creatures in them. Once, He took me to the sea to name each of them. Some of the whales and fish are enormous, far bigger than our turtles. It's as blue as the sky, and the farther you descend, the darker it becomes until it's almost pitch-black like the night."

She imagined being surrounded by a vista of the purest blue. "Endless waters," she repeated. "Will I ever be able to visit them?"

Adam shrugged. "One day, when Father tells us to go, we'll go. Until then, we have our work to do, and our hill at night to enjoy." He winked at her, his grin flashing white and charming—an invitation to play, and so much more.

She swam away from him, focusing on her arms and legs pumping together as one. At least swimming kept her from responding. Adam always gave the same answers, no matter how often she pressed. Perhaps she differed from him with these longings to see beyond the garden. Perhaps as the serpent noted, she was truly the curious one. As she reached the edge of the lake, Adam caught up with her with easy strokes. Beneath both of them, turtles dived and chased each other, as if eager to play. But she had had enough of playing.

She climbed out of the water and ran her hands down her long hair, squeezing out the excess water from each curled strand. Beneath the sun, her skin and hair would dry soon. Adam trudged out of the lake but not before waving to the turtles. He almost seemed disappointed to leave them, but he settled beside her on the sunbaked grass.

"What if we leave the garden just for a day or two and came back?" she asked. Perhaps this might be another option to explore.

"When Father tells me, then I will go. One day, our children will fill the entire earth. Believe me, Woman, we will have all of eternity to explore all that He has made. Why not savor this moment right now?"

His answer brought a curious sensation of feeling suppressed. The turtles eased out of the water and flopped onto the banks to sun themselves. Soon, several of them fell asleep while butterflies fluttered on top of their hardened shells.

Even Adam lay down and closed his eyes, basking in the sunlight. All around her, Eden moved with a rhythm of rest, as if everything in it chose a slower pace. Or, perhaps, the animals copied Adam. The cycles were increasingly clear to her. Eat, drink, work, rest. Play.

A breath escaped her as the world around her slowed while bumblebees sleepily dropped into the nearest roses to suck nectar. Adam's chest rose and fell, but as for her? Relaxation was impossible, especially with this mounting restless feeling inside of her. Wrapping her arms around her legs, she laid her head on top of her knees while the beauty and wonder around her went unnoticed.

Was the serpent right? Could she choose her own path of freedom?

In the garden's hush, when her thoughts were free to roam, how easily her imagination drifted back to the forbidden tree. It stood in the center of her mind, digging its deep and gnarled roots into her spirit. The sharp prickle that usually warned her not to think such thoughts dimmed. And as the sun warmed her shoulders and back, a picture of the bluish tree easily formed in her mind. She could see herself taking that fruit and an explosion of light bursting from her fingertips, like the creation story Adam had shared.

Why had God made her so curious? She simply couldn't shake the desire to know more.

Should she talk to Father about her troubling desire? It was far easier to brush aside the notion. Instead, she lay down on the grass next to Adam and pictured the tree once again.

By the time evening came, she had a complete idea of what Adam viewed as rest. They raced with deer through the meadows.

Together, they swam again in the river, allowing the refreshing current to pull them until they nearly reached the border of Eden. They climbed the highest hill of the garden and watched stars twinkle brilliantly in the sky.

"What would you like to do?" he asked her, as if eager to know her thoughts and draw her from her new silence. Then he nuzzled her neck, planting kisses there along her skin, "What can I do to make you smile?"

"I have you and Father," she answered, reaching for his hand to entwine her fingers with his. "And it's been a lovely day."

The adoring look Adam flashed her brought a wave of happiness. But only for a moment. She stood on the hill observing the sunlight, while Adam settled down for the night.

Daughter, did you have a good day? her Father's voice asked in her mind, a quiet whisper to the churning of her thoughts.

She nodded, folding her arms across her chest.

I have so much planned for you, My child. Be patient. It's coming. I want you to know that I desire the very best for you. I love you.

"I love You too, Father," she said under her breath.

Instead of lingering to chat with Him as she had, she made the excuse that she was tired. Father's enveloping presence retreated, giving her space. Crickets chirped and a wolf sang as the moon drifted in the sky.

A heavy sigh rattled through her. Perhaps she should join Adam and sleep. Perhaps in the morning, she would feel much better.

Really, she ought to be content with her life as things stood. After all, she had Adam and Eden, and her Father too. She had plenty of fascinating things to do and to enjoy. But there was a sense of something more, just beyond her reach, as distant as the horizon, which always fled the closer she moved toward it. Something more she wanted and she could not rest until she discovered it.

A hiss drew her attention to the outstretched tree.

"You saw a white serpent?" Adam joined her as the sunrise crested over the horizon.

Resisting the urge to smooth his wild but charming locks, she paused from peeling the array of oranges she had picked for the morning meal and nodded her answer. The serpent had disappeared as soon as she moved aside a branch—the action puzzling.

"In our tree, on the top of our hill?" he asked again.

It was endearing how Adam kept referring to the hill they slept on as their hill. A shared and sacred space to call their own. In the late evening and early dawn, when the dew watered the ground and a low rolling fog crept over the meadow and river, she and Adam remained on the high ground, dry and warm.

He rubbed his chin as he glanced toward the branches that offered a shady canopy during the day. "That would be a first. I've never seen a white serpent. I'll have to think of a special name for it."

She handed him a peeled orange. "I knew I should have awakened you."

The sparkle in his eyes as he took the orange brought another flush of pleasure to her cheeks and neck. "Woman, you can wake me for any reason, especially for a new animal."

When they had finished eating, Adam went to their tree and examined it. She waited patiently as he brushed aside the foliage, just as she had done under the cover of night. Shaking his head, he recaptured her hand in his, raising it long enough to press a kiss to her knuckles.

"Maybe we will find it later. I want to check on the sheep first."

She walked beside him down the trail, past the river running beside the meadow, where sheep had gathered together. His grip, not too tight, not too loose, swung her hand back and forth between them.

In her mind, the mysterious serpent darted away, just out of her grasp. His challenge lingered with her. Why indeed, would God forbid such a remarkable thing to gather more knowledge and to become more like Him?

Adam glanced at her, his green eyes darkening. He playfully nudged her with his shoulder. "You are unusually silent this morning. You know, I do believe I miss your chatter. It reminds me of the chirping bluebirds who sing with the rising dawn."

Dare she tell him she still wondered about the purple fruit? Biting her lip, she focused on her steps. "I see many lambs this morning."

He released his grip on her and hurried to the nearest ewe with its newborn lamb. Kneeling beside the sheep, he let his fingers skim the head of the lamb and its pale pink ears covered with white fluff. "Father will be so pleased. He commanded we all be fruitful and multiply to fill the earth. Everywhere I look, I see new life. I wonder how many sheep there are?"

To her surprise, Adam counted out loud, gesturing with his arm as he pinpointed each newborn creature, a ball of white wool hidden in the fragrant grass and wildflowers. The numbers were a new concept to her. And the sheep all looked the same, but Adam appeared to know each one by sight, easily recalling the smallest details.

"Did you create these words too?" she asked.

Adam shook his head. "Father taught me about numbers. It was easier to count when I named each of the animals. I remember everything I see, including everything I hear. But His abilities far outshine mine. Did you know that He had no beginning, unlike us? No beginning and no end."

She folded her arms across her chest. "Did someone make Him?"

"No." Adam paused, counting to answer. "He alone is the Creator, living in a heavenly realm with his servants, the angels."

A curious sensation settled in her. Adam knew so much more than she did. Of course, she wasn't certain how long he had been alone with Father until her arrival, speaking of all these different issues, but it was undeniable that Adam's knowledge currently surpassed her own.

They continued walking through the meadow, tallying the numbers as they passed the lambs and ewes. The numbers climbed higher and higher, but her mind had no trouble keeping up with Adam's counting. Before she realized it, she had drifted far past the meadow, closer and closer to the heart of Eden.

A few lambs bounced on unsteady legs, skipping through the grass to the north of the meadow. One of them squeezed through a cascading series of vines forming a barrier, only to have its hind leg ensnared by one stubborn vine. With a chuckle, she darted after the lamb, her legs pumping. Adam would at least have an accurate count if she retrieved the mischievous lamb.

Besides, it felt good to stretch her muscles. Her chest pounded with a heady rhythm, and her speed had improved, sending her nearly flying across the dirt.

She heard Adam's voice call out to her. Raising her hand to signal where she was headed, she continued forward until she reached the forested area, dripping in more sturdy vines and brush. The lamb wiggled free of the thicket just as she reached it. With a huff of laughter, she brushed aside the dense foliage and the wide ferns, her toes sinking into the damp soil. There the tiny lamb stood, bleating, as if pleased to play a game.

She reached it with a few strides, scooping up the warm body into her arms, and pressed a kiss against its head. "Found you."

But when she raised her head, another sight collided with her gaze. The two mighty trees, one tall and one squat, waited near the gurgling river. As she lowered the lamb to the ground, ignoring its bleating protest at leaving the safety of her arms, she found herself unable to return to her beloved.

For one long moment, she stared at the Tree of Knowledge of Good and Evil. When she glanced at her feet, the lamb was gone. A swift look over her shoulder revealed no sign of Adam. She was all alone.

Again, a sense of heaviness tugged at her, repelling and inviting at once, reviving her old curiosity. It wasn't wrong to look, was it? She could walk the perimeter around the tree and keep a careful distance from it. Father couldn't object to that, could He? After all, He had brought her to the tree. He had even rustled the leaves with His breeze, proving that He, at least, could draw close enough to touch it.

Besides, she loved the garden and the plants. She might even learn something if she studied it closer. She didn't have to touch it or eat anything. Just one quick look to satisfy her questions…

Inhaling a sharp breath, she took a step forward and another, until at last she could almost stand on tiptoes and reach the lowest of the hanging fruit. Waxy leaves barely moved in the rippling wind. The sense of heaviness increased the longer she stood beneath the outstretched branches shading her from the brilliant sun. Despite the warning prickles running along her arms and back, Eve saw that the tree appeared very ordinary and safe up close. Far more ordinary than when she had observed it from the safe distance with her Father.

A slither from above warned her that she was no longer alone. She raised her head, and there, the elusive white serpent unfolded itself from a bluish branch.

"It's you," she breathed in wonder as she reached out to brush her fingers against it. To her delight, the serpent uncurled from the branch and crept toward her, nudging his head into her hand just like the darling lambs. "I wondered when I would see you again. I think I shall call you Star Light, for you shine like the stars in the evening sky."

It had been Adam's habit to converse with the animals, and as a result, she had copied him, chatting happily to the deer and the birds and anything else that would listen.

"How brave you are to come to this tree. I had hoped that you would visit me." The serpent closed his eyes and purred with something akin to delight.

"I didn't mean to come here," she said. "You see, there was a lamb that ran away from me, and the lambs like to play games...."

The serpent almost seemed to smile as he slid along the branch, moving closer to her with those great blinking eyes and flickering tongue. "How kind of you to watch over those poor creatures. They're not as bright as you, are they?"

"You said you are different because you ate from the tree. Why haven't you died as Father promised?"

He didn't immediately answer as he jiggled the branch so that the nearest purple fruit appeared as if it would drop onto her head. Alarmed, she held out her hand to catch the fruit just in case it fell.

The serpent halted just above her. "Make no mistake, I *am* different. Much like you, I suspect. I was curious too. But you are asking the wrong questions. Why would your loving Father threaten death for something so simple as you eating from this tree? Why doesn't He trust you?"

She stared at him for a moment longer. How to answer such a question? Father's command no longer made as much sense as it once did.

A ray of sun broke through the shadow of the tree, highlighting the serpent's gorgeous scales. His silver body broke into a myriad of colors: pale blue, pink, and yellow. She had seen nothing quite so mesmerizing, other than the tree of course.

"I just wanted to see the tree up close. That's all. I'm not here to eat its fruit or—"

"Woman, you won't die. I promise," the serpent interrupted her, his voice so kind and…so fatherly. "You'll be freer than you've ever been. The entire world will be yours to explore, and you won't have to wait. You'll do as you please, when you please. Trust me."

Her mouth opened and closed as she considered what was offered. Adam had told her the very first day to trust him when trying the avocado. Something filled her, something that made her want to jump and run from the restless feeling within her. It didn't seem right to place that tree right there in the middle of the garden where all would eventually encounter it. How could she continually avoid such a spot? Or her children, for that matter? Besides, it was all she could think about right now. Father had told her she had the ability to choose, but it didn't feel fair.

After all, why shouldn't she have a taste of what it would feel like to be a god? To soar with sheer power and wisdom rippling through her body and mind, as glorious as the sun and the moon? To touch the stars and decide what her fate would be?

All she was asking was for a taste. She didn't need to eat the entire fruit—just a small nibble and then discover…

She could control what happened to her with one nibble, right? She could stop before things got out of hand. Why couldn't she be all-knowing like Him? Especially if He made her? Surely such a desire wasn't wrong. It was fruit, after all. The mango she ate brought nothing but pleasure. Why would He deny her this extra joy?

A heady sensation filled her, and the branch lowered, shifting the fruit within reach as the serpent resettled his weight on it. The fruit smelled like plums. Ripe plums dripping with fragrant juice. And plums had never killed her. She stood on her tiptoes and peered closer. The waxy texture of the leaves coated the purple skin. Different. Intriguing.

And yes, she wanted more knowledge. She wanted all of it. Why should she wait?

She reached out to finger the skin of the fruit just as Adam shouted in the distance.

CHAPTER FIVE

The serpent slid back into the trees while she waited beneath the branches of the forbidden tree. Adam jogged toward her, his smile diminished. She withdrew from the purple fruit, suddenly self-conscious.

"I looked everywhere for you," he said as he shoved his hand through his thick locks.

"The lamb ran away, and I found myself at the tree," she replied, hiding her hands behind her back as an awkward silence loomed between them.

"We should return before evening falls," he said, glancing over his shoulder to the meadow—just as she had done only moments prior. Only a meek breeze rustled through the leaves. No sign of her Father's presence.

Adam looked at her, his thick brows lowered a second time when she didn't reply.

How could she possibly leave, especially following the white serpent's challenge, which continued to reverberate inside of her?

"I found the white serpent. He is here, in this very tree, and he lives, despite having touched the tree. I believe he ate the fruit and survived."

At her mention, the serpent peeked through the bluish leaves.

Adam gasped.

"He talks, Adam. Truly speaks as we do. He assured me that we will not die if we eat of the fruit of this tree."

Adam appeared unconvinced. He folded his arms across his broad chest. "I don't believe it."

She flushed, wavering with indecision. Who spoke the truth? The serpent or her Father?

The serpent lowered himself from a stout branch. "Perhaps you misheard God. He can be rather rigid in His ideas. A shame, really."

Adam's eyes widened, and he took a step backward. "How is this possible? I've never heard an animal speak before."

"Your God wants complete power for Himself, I fear," the snake answered with his tongue flickering. "If only He was more open-minded about sharing His glory and power with others. But, alas, He likes to be first in all things."

"See!" She gestured toward the white snake uncoiling around the branch. "What if Father was wrong? What if we can eat of the tree and gain more wisdom?"

Perhaps her Father truly had the best intentions, but He was far too careful in guarding His creation. What if she proved to Him that she could endure a bite from the Tree of Knowledge of Good and Evil? That she was strong and smart enough to handle whatever came her way.

To her surprise, Adam said nothing as she moved closer to the fruit and slowly placed her hand on it, yet she couldn't help but notice how his chest heaved with deep breaths. Had he changed his mind? Was he too questioning whether Father was right?

With a smile to reassure Adam, she pulled on the nearest fruit, yanking it free from the branch. Encouraged by his silence and the flexing of his jaw, as if he too wondered as she had, she held it out to him to show the wrinkled skin. He watched her, his eyes as round as the moon.

The sound of rapid breathing and the trees rattling their branches filled the silence between them. She deliberately raised the fruit to her mouth, paused for just the briefest fraction, and then bit into the fruit to prove it was safe.

Adam lurched forward, placing his hand on her shoulder. "Woman!"

She ignored his reaction. The fruit had very little juice in it. The thick flesh tasted like the fig she had sampled the day prior. Chewy but sweet. Very, very sweet. So sweet…

She offered him the rest of it. "I'm still here, Adam. See? I'm perfectly fine."

He visibly gulped. With a look of agony, he stared at her and then at the serpent.

"Wouldn't you like to know what you are missing?" The serpent's pale tongue darted in and out of his mouth. "Don't let her eat that fruit alone. You'll be separated forever if you don't act immediately."

With trembling fingers, Adam raised the fruit to his mouth and sank his teeth into the purple skin. It was a small bite. Unlike hers. A nibble, really.

He seemed to chew it, swallowing it as if it were a hard lump, his throat bobbing with the action.

Faint laughter, full of mockery and malice, echoed from the tree. But it was enough to send a stab of something awful through her. *She knew what malice was.* The sweetness on her tongue became something bitter and acidic, while her stomach roiled strangely, threatening to send everything clawing back up her throat.

He lied! The serpent had *lied* to her. Instead of exploding with light and power, her mind was threaded with tendrils of darkness and misery. They rippled through her, rendering her weak and shaking. It was if her body had changed at its core. Her thoughts. Her very essence.

No, her mind screamed. *This can't be happening.*

She placed her hand on her stomach to calm it, only to see her breasts…her legs…her naked body, as naked as could be. Startled, she raised her head to stare at Adam, who wiped his mouth with the back of his hand. He froze, his gaze trapped on her exposed form. Then he whirled around, presenting her with his backside. But not before she saw everything as well.

Oh…

He was naked too.

"O God—" His voice came out strangled. "What have I done?" With all his strength, he hurled the hateful fruit into the river. Then, without even looking at her, he darted toward the thick foliage, leaving her behind, frozen next to the Tree of Knowledge of Good and Evil.

She tried to cover her body with her hands and failed. "Adam—wait! Please! Don't leave me!"

But he ignored her as he ran into the copse of trees and dense vines. At his loud rustling, a flock of birds scattered in every direction, taking flight far above him, to far safer heights.

The birds avoided Adam.

All at once, a new awakening dawned within her, and it was terrifying to behold. She knew what was good and what was evil. The serpent, for one, was evil. Without a doubt, he had tricked her, but for what purpose?

It didn't matter in the end.

There was only one thing that mattered now, and she feared she had ruined everything with her actions. Did God know what she had done?

She trudged into the forest, searching for leaves large enough to cover her body.

Some fronds were long and wide, spanning the length of her forearm. If she took a few of the sturdier vines, she might pierce the skin of the fig leaves and string something together to cover her exposed front and backside. It was worth a try. She was certainly desperate.

And very much alone, at the moment.

The sun had begun its descent, touching everything with a vulgar crimson light. Shuddering, she ripped off a vine and tugged at a few of the largest leaves closest to her. With shaking hands, she assembled a clumsy covering that did nothing to hide her form, using fronds and fig leaves, or whatever was nearest to her.

All the while, Adam's horrified gaze when he saw her naked circled over and over in her mind. Just thinking about it made her feel the flush of disgust. How many times prior to the forbidden fruit had he glanced at her, exulting in her beauty? Her body hadn't changed. But now, part of her wanted to jump in the river and wash away the stain of his repulsion, but no doubt there was nothing she could do to scrub away the grime she felt inside her spirit.

A crashing sound through the brush brought a tension to her shoulders as she braced herself to see her Father. Desperate to escape, she pivoted on her feet, tripping on an exposed root of a tree trunk and falling to the ground with a thud.

Her knee ached from the impact. When had the ground turned so hard? Before, it had cushioned her feet and form, as comforting as an embrace. With a cry, she clutched her leg, alarmed to see her skin scratched and raw, with tiny pebbles embedded into her knee.

A hand reached out for her, and with a startled squeak, she tried to shrink into herself as if she could make herself disappear.

Adam grabbed her arm and roughly yanked her to her feet.

He glared at her, his green eyes narrowed to mere slits. "Why, Woman? Why did you eat of the tree and leave me no choice but to eat as well?"

Her mind moved too sluggishly to keep up with his anger as he continued to stare at her with such rage. A muscle ticked in his jaw, and his fingers, always gentle, now pinched her upper arm until she hurt.

"Let go of me," she rasped. "If you are so concerned, why didn't you try to stop me from eating it? You stood there and did absolutely nothing! Not one peep from you as you watched me take it."

"You moved so quickly, there wasn't anything I do to stop you. I couldn't…couldn't imagine myself without you, so I did it too. Does that make you satisfied?" He immediately released his grip, but her arm ached. "Father will know we've disobeyed."

His answer didn't ring quite true, nor did it comfort her to hear him wish to be with her.

"But the serpent said we wouldn't die." As soon as she said it, she felt foolish. A wave of ugly emotions crested within her—too many to discern. She felt like yelling. Stamping her foot or smashing something. Anything to escape what was boiling inside of her, ready to erupt into a spew of agony.

Adam ran a palm down his face but not before she saw a curl to his upper lip. "Obviously, he *lied*."

She couldn't help but notice he now wore a ridiculous design of palm fronds fastened around his narrow hips. Blushing, she quickly glanced away before he noticed her gaping at his exposed legs.

"What will Father do now?"

With a sigh, Adam sank down onto the ground. "I don't know what He'll do. He told us clearly not to eat of the tree, and now we've both broken His one rule."

One rule. She hadn't been able to follow one rule, and worse, Adam evidently blamed her for the transgression.

"Maybe He won't notice that we ate of the tree. Maybe nothing will change," she protested weakly.

But that, too, was false. Curse this knowledge whispering rebuttals in her mind every time she tried to defend herself. Already, she realized the consequences of her choice. The world around her was changing moment by moment, like the darkness ascending within her. A shadow had leaked over all the garden, staining everything in its path. The butterflies that settled on her shoulder during the day now floated in the breeze, keeping their distance from her. And the birds remained high in the sky, with wings outspread to catch the upper currents, while the garden remained eerily silent, without song or movement. Most of the animals took refuge, hidden in greenery.

She sank down onto the ground, numb and exhausted. All her body craved was sleep.

Adam shifted his form so his broad back was to her. He remained that way for the rest of the evening, locked inside a sullen silence. Despite their previously heated words, that awful silence grew between them, cold and foreboding. She bit the inside of her cheek until it throbbed as she swallowed all the things she wanted to say.

Neither of them ate anything. Nor did she or Adam return to their beloved hill. And as evening fell with a disturbing weight, she heard a familiar rustle above her head, one that brought a sickening sensation to her stomach.

A flash of glittering white from a long sinuous body, and then the serpent was gone.

CHAPTER SIX

"Wake up." A hand roughly jostled her from a terrifying dream. "Wake up, now."

She sat up, rubbing her eyes from sleep, only to see Adam's shocked expression right in front of hers.

"Please," he whispered close to her ear, his hot breath fanning her cheeks, "I hear Father walking in the garden. He's headed in our direction."

She shot up from the hard ground, alarm coursing through her body. Adam reached his arm around her waist and pulled her close to him. The action brought a strange ache to her chest. She had slept alone, plagued with horrible visions of him abandoning her on their hill while the world around her dissolved into dust and decay.

Every muscle in her body ached, but the sound of the wind rushing through the trees forced her to hasten. Adam pointed silently to a thicket where they could hide. She obeyed, crawling on her hands and knees, scooting beneath the canopy as fast as she could. He grunted as he slid in place, pulling giant ferns to further hide them.

"Adam. Woman. Where are you?" Father called out as His mighty voice stirred the ferns surrounding her. "I've come to walk with you today. Come and show Me where you are."

A groan escaped Adam as he shook beside her. She clenched her teeth tightly to keep them from chattering. Everything within her wanted to cry out to her Father. *Here I am. Your daughter.* But how could she utter those words now, after all that had happened? What would He say—or, worse, *do*—when He discovered what she had done?

She had disobeyed the Almighty God who had made the heavens and the earth. Truly, she would be mere dust, just like her nightmares, crushed within His hands if He so chose.

"Adam, why do you hide from Me? Woman, why won't you show Me your face?" How sad and hurt her Father sounded as a breeze gathered strength, rippling through the branches overhead. Flower petals scattered in the breeze, seeping through the thicket to cover her dirty toes.

He knew where they lay hidden.

"We can't remain here," Adam said in a low tone. He thrust aside the ferns and scrambled out of the thicket, raising his voice to be heard. "I heard You in the garden, and I was afraid because I was naked, so I hid."

She edged out slowly, trying to conceal her body as she stood beside her partner.

The breeze came to a halt and then swirled around both of them, bringing a cascade of bruised petals to float around her and Adam. It was as if the invisible hand of God stirred the soil and air, refusing to let them run away a second time.

"Who told you that you were naked? Have you eaten from the tree that I commanded you not to?"

Adam pinched his lips tightly together for a moment. "The woman you put here with me—she gave me some fruit from the tree, and I ate it."

He kept his eyes averted from her. She sucked in a sharp breath, her lungs throbbing at the betrayal. Why did Adam blame her? He was just as much at fault as she was. The breeze briefly touched her face, but instead of bringing comfort, she wanted to run away as fast as she could.

"What is this you have done?" her Father asked. He sounded as if He were about to weep.

Skin aflame and her mouth dry, she stuttered out an answer. "The serpent deceived me, and I ate."

The breeze became a whirlwind, snagging pebbles, leaves, flowers, and sticks off the ground. A righteous anger seemed to vibrate through the wind as it picked up speed, lifting her hair high above her head. She covered her face with her hands.

She felt rather than heard God command the serpent. *Come here.*

When she dared to peek between her fingers, to her shock, the white serpent slunk from the nearest tree. A shiver rippled down her spine when she realized he had spent the night hovering above her and Adam, as if to keep watch, or to stalk them.

He pattered on small legs, his silver scales far less beautiful in the morning light. The frill hung limply about his neck, and he lowered his head until it nearly grazed the ground.

"Because you have done this, cursed are you above all livestock and all wild animals! You will crawl on your belly, and you will eat dust all the days of your life. And I will put enmity between you and the woman, and between your offspring and hers; he will crush your head, and you will strike his heel." The wind shifted from her and centered on the serpent.

To her astonishment, the reptile writhed on the ground, an anguished scream pouring from his rigid mouth. His small legs withered, leaving him to flop helplessly before sliding away into the dirt.

Perhaps more chilling, the silver light in his eyes turned oily black. Had something else seeped from the serpent?

"Woman—" The deep voice drew her back to the whirlwind, which slowed, drawing a circle around her in the dirt. She shuddered, dreading what God would say next.

He did not leave her guessing.

"I will make your pains in childbearing very severe. With painful labor you will give birth to children. Your desire will be for your husband, and he will rule over you."

Then, God moved the wind to Adam, drawing the same circle around him. "Because you listened to your wife and ate fruit from the tree about which I commanded you, 'You must not eat from it,'. Cursed is the ground because of you; through painful toil you will eat food from it all the days of your life. It will produce thorns and thistles for you, and you will eat the plants in the field. By the sweat of your brow you will eat your food until you return to the ground, since from it you were taken, for dust you are and to dust you will return."

She gasped at the finality of the words as Adam groaned audibly. The fig leaves fluttered away from them, flimsy coverings that couldn't withstand the force of the whirlwind.

"Wait here until I find suitable clothing for you both." There was a sharp edge to her Father's voice, loud enough that the trees swayed, rattling their branches, sending another shower of leaves to scatter.

And then, in an instant, the wind subsided, leaving only an unnatural silence in the foliage. The only sounds came from Adam pacing back and forth and her own harsh breathing.

Adam wore a path in the dirt with his frantic steps. When his gaze snagged on hers and dropped to her form, she hurriedly folded her arms across her chest.

A shriek echoed from the lush forest. Unnatural and loud and full of agony.

Adam halted, his eyes nearly bulging and his fists clenched at his side.

"What it is it, Adam? What happened out there to make that dreadful sound?"

"I don't know. I can't hear Father in my thoughts anymore. He's shut me out."

Her as well. No longer did God speak in her mind. In vain she tried to reach out with her thoughts to call Him, but no answer came back to her. The inner silence was deafening. They both waited, hardly daring to breathe lest that sound echo again.

How could she ever forget such a hideous cry?

"Come and see what I have brought you." God's audible voice shook her from her twisting thoughts.

She and Adam left the safety of the copse of trees and crept toward the meadow, where two brown flaps lay spread out across the grass. At first, her mind struggled to understand what she saw. But Adam reached the items first and gagged, holding a fist over his mouth. Water flooded his eyes as he shook his head violently.

"Adam, there is always a cost when you disobey. It isn't just you who will suffer but those around you. This is but one consequence of your choice," God said. "I killed these animals on your behalf. You will need these tunics in the days to come. Take and wear them."

She knelt on the ground and touched the smaller of the pieces, a tunic with a hole for her head and two side holes for her arms. A garment far more secure than her ridiculous fig leaves, which continued to shed until nothing would be left.

Dressing herself felt so strange as she held the tunic in her hands and pulled it over her head. With a few tugs, it settled onto her hips, falling past her knees. Unlike her clumsy threading of vines and fig leaves, a fine stitching with some thin strip of material held the skins together. The tunic was dry and smooth, but it felt strange rubbing against her skin and under her armpits and around her neck. Part of her missed the freedom of no clothes, yet she could never return to such a state.

Adam dressed silently. But as he straightened his garment, a ragged sigh escaped him.

Their punishment wasn't over, however.

Her Father's last warning would prove even more devastating. "Because you have become like one of Us, knowing good and evil, you may not reach out your hand and take from the Tree of Life and live forever. Eden will no longer be your home. And I will no longer walk with either of you."

She and Adam fled Eden with only the animal skins as a covering. Following the river to the place of the tributaries, they scurried past the meadow, past their beloved rounded hill with its outstretched tree for cover, past the meadow with the white flowers, and out of the garden.

None of the animals followed Adam. Indeed, they hid or slunk away at the sight of the two of them. Adam groaned again when the herd of deer ran fleet-footed away from him, moving as one. None of the lambs he oversaw during the birthing process approached him. No birds trilled music from the trees. It was as if everything that had life knew that death had entered into the world, and now they too feared it.

To her shock, as she passed swaths of familiar flowers, more leaves and petals began to brown and wilt as though a shadow fell over them. She stumbled to keep up with Adam's furious pace. He paused long enough to wrap a hard arm about her waist. His brow furrowed when he slanted a look at her. "I fear we cannot linger in the garden any longer, or we will die. Can you make it just a little farther? If we follow the path of the river, hopefully we'll find a place to rest by nightfall."

She nodded. Her lungs ached and her head swam. Somehow, it felt as though she were walking underwater, each step taking so much more effort than she ever remembered. Ahead, the gentle river emptied into the four tributaries at the Eastern entrance. All around the garden, a rocky formation stretched in every direction, keeping the garden separate from the rest of the world. At long last, she would discover what lay beyond Eden's boundaries. But dread filled her. How curious that the horizon she spent hours watching no longer had the power to move her. Instead, she swiveled to look over her shoulder, to gaze upon her home one last time and remember all that she had lost.

To her shock, a pair of floating lights circled high in the air before zooming downward to merge at the entrance of Eden where the river flowed. The lights stretched and glimmered, taking the form of a manlike creature with four white wings flared out, spanning the entire distance between the rock walls. The being, covered with silver eyes, stared at her without emotion. In his massive hands, he held something aloft, sharp and piercing, the metal glinting beneath the sunlight, while the river below him reflected his brilliance.

A cry escaped Adam, and the being followed the sound, revealing four heads set upon its massive shoulders. A man, an ox, a lion, and an eagle.

She cowered at the magnificent sight of such purity and holiness, qualities she had tossed aside with little thought. More lights gathered strength, each one merging into different winged apparitions. They spread out with the first angel, and as they tilted their heads to stare at her, their faces, comprised of animal and man, jutted outward from different angles from each form. Their legs straightened and lengthened until they touched the river, but the soles of their feet were like the sole of a calf's foot, glittering like the veins of yellow metal in Eden. Even the angel with the features of a man appeared to glow hotter and hotter, giving her a glimpse of a reality so terrifying, she would have collapsed to her knees had not Adam caught her arm and jerked her upright.

Holy, holy, holy, they seemed to say in a hum that vibrated the air she breathed. *Holy is the Lord God Almighty*. The hum became a roar, hurting her ears until they rang.

She was no longer worthy of being associated with such righteousness.

Dead silence fell, more awful than the angelic song.

"The angel with a flaming sword—it is one of the cherubim." Adam sounded winded beside her. She glanced briefly at him. Horror lined his face when he shifted to meet her gaze. "We can never return to Eden. They will kill us or our children if we try to cross the threshold."

Flames pulsated along the entire blade. She felt the searing heat from the angels and stepped backward. Adam shuffled as well, edging to the left of her. The flaming sword swelled in size to fill the gap between the wall of rock enclosing the garden. Like a living thing, it tracked left, as if sensing Adam's small footsteps. When she moved right, it swiveled, casting a blistering heat in her direction.

There would be no way to sneak back into the garden. The angels and the rotating sword would ensure the Tree of Life's safety.

As the angelic beings faded from view, the intensity of the sword still scorched the air.

"Come." Adam tugged her forward into the harsh unknown. The muscle in his jaw bunched as he faced the wide swath of unfamiliar land that lay before Eden. "We must hurry."

CHAPTER SEVEN

By the time night fell, she had walked and walked and walked until her feet ached. Toes swollen and leg muscles cramping, she struggled to get enough air into her throbbing lungs before taking one more step. And then another. Would they ever stop walking? The sky remained the same as always, faintly mocking her as the nearly full moon rose to illuminate a strange path.

But the world had changed. The wind no longer felt like a caress against her cheeks. The ground had hardened into something unwelcoming and ugly, littered with dying foliage or twigs. Nothing edible grew along the way. How could she forget the luscious apples or oranges that she had left behind in Eden?

Stomach growling, she pressed her arm against her middle to quell the sound. Exhaustion pressed down on her as Adam guided her past the river where moonlight limned the rushing surface. She tripped and fell against him. He pulled her upright against his cold frame, his gaze concerned. "We'll rest for the night. I don't think you can walk any farther."

She wanted to protest and keep walking, especially considering all that she had done. It was the least she could do. Surely her suffering feet couldn't compare to the distress mounting within her, threatening to rip her apart.

Before she could protest, a lone howl echoed in the distance, bloodcurdling and mournful all at once.

Adam's features hardened to stone. "I think I see shelter." He nodded toward a swath of shadows, which, upon closer examination, revealed the narrow opening to a cave.

Limping, she tried to keep pace with him as he scrambled over moss-covered rocks, his grip secure around her waist. Inside the cramped space, the air felt cool and damp, but it smelled strange. Awful, in truth. She sank to the rocky ground, trying to ignore the pain in her stomach and the sharp pebbles digging into her skin. When had she last eaten? Whenever she had been hungry in Eden, she had simply taken what she needed. Now how would she find food in this ruthless landscape? A slight cry escaped her.

He raised her chin with his finger, his eyes unreadable in the dim light. "I'll find something to eat for both of us. I want you to stay here where it is safer."

She was about to protest when the howl reverberated across the river a second time.

He placed a warning finger on her lips and stood. Before she could protest, he crept out of the opening, moving noiselessly in the dark.

Wrapping her arms about her knees, she waited for his return. Her breathing quickened in the long absence. What if he abandoned her, just as she had seen in that dreadful nightmare? What if he left her as Father had?

Perhaps she deserved to be abandoned, considering all she had done.

A blood-curdling roar stole the breath out of her lungs. Gasping for air, she crawled on her hands and knees to the entrance of the cave. Did she dare go after Adam? Where was he? In vain, she tried to pierce the heavy gloom as the thick clouds obscured the silver moon.

"Adam!" she cried out, unable to hold her fear. "Adam!"

A scream answered. Startling and sharp, it sounded like him.

She covered her mouth with her hands and groaned silently.

"Father, please help him," she whispered. But no audible answer came to her. No reassuring breeze. Instead, a harsh wind, devoid of Father's presence, picked up pace, whipping past the cave entrance with an eerie moan. She was about to leave to search for Adam when a hulking form, grunting with effort, slid into the cave.

"You came back." Her voice sounded weak.

Her husband didn't answer immediately as he cradled something in his arms.

"Adam?"

"I didn't find food, but I found a lamb," he said tightly. "It's hurt. A wolf and a lion were fighting over it before I chased them away."

The lamb barely bleated when she touched it.

Carefully, Adam set it on the ground. "I don't know if it will survive the night. When I found it, its leg had been broken." He sounded equally broken, as if his throat was raw with strain and grief. "I rescued it just in time. I think the lion would have eaten both wolf and lamb if given the chance."

A strangled sob welled up within her, and suddenly, liquid poured from her eyes, dripping down to her chin. All of this wretchedness because of one bite of the forbidden fruit?

"Woman!" he exclaimed as he placed a palm against her cheek.

She wept so hard she couldn't speak. Emotions exploded within her—and in the seasons to come, she would understand each one and give them names. Grief, shame, guilt, and despair. Hopelessness and fear. Panic too.

He pulled her close to him and slanted his mouth over hers. The kiss seared her—there was an urgency to it, a desperation she had never experienced before. When he finally released her, she shuddered.

"You didn't think I would leave you, did you?"

"I didn't know what to think anymore," she whispered as she attempted to study him despite the darkness. "Everything's.... changed. But mostly, I feared I would lose you one way or another when I heard that roar."

Yet, here in the safety of his arms, she might pretend that the garden hadn't happened. That he loved her as he once did—her sweet Adam with the charming grin carving a dimple into his left cheek. But there was nothing gentle about the arms banded around her waist. Even so, he was tender when he finally spoke.

"Flesh of my flesh and bone of my bone. We are one and always will be. I vow that I will always take care of you and come back to you." He rested his forehead against hers. "From now on, I will call you Eve, the mother of all living."

When she lay down, cradling the lamb while Adam held her, she tasted the new name in her mind. *Eve.* The mother of all living.

She didn't deserve this name. Not when so much of this was her fault. Hadn't she broken the very paradise that God had given her? Hadn't she ruined everything?

How could she possibly want to bring a precious child into this dark and dangerous world?

When Eve woke, she discovered Adam had collected a giant frond filled with blueberries. The fruit waited for her in a small mound, nestled carefully inside the leaf. Tears flooded her eyes again when she glanced at the precious offering left during the early quiet of the dawn. Not only had he brought her the fruit, he had kept it from getting dirty from the cave floor.

She tasted the berries, surprised when the tart, sweet flavor still hit her tongue. At least some goodness remained. Her hunger flared again after she finished her share, but she would have to make do with the supply she had. Besides, so much work awaited her. She scarcely knew what to tackle first.

The lamb barely raised its head when she approached it. To her surprise, Adam had retrieved vines and had snapped a sturdy branch, creating a brace to stabilize the misshapen leg.

How had she not heard him awaken? How tired she must have been to have slept so soundly! Shame heated her cheeks.

She resolved to leave him most of the berries since his appetite far surpassed hers, even when living in Eden.

The sun had already crested, illuminating the river and another dense forest canopy to the west. When she stepped outside the cave, she shielded her eyes from the brilliant light. Adam limped toward her. He swung a stout stick in his hand, wielding it almost like the angel with his sword.

"I've found a patch of meadow in the nearby forest," Adam said when he saw her. "We are close to the river for water, and we can forage for berries and other food. I say we stay and harvest this land."

She noted the dark circles beneath his eyes. The long, oozing scratch on his leg, however, demanded her immediate attention.

Fear filled her again as she bent to study it closer. "When did you get hurt?"

He waved her away but not without leaning on the stick. "The lion lashed out at me with its claws. For a moment, I thought it would kill me, but it ran away at the last moment. Or maybe it ate the wolf and did not need to eat me. I searched for the wolf, but I couldn't find it this morning."

Bile rose in the back of her throat. "The animals kill each other now."

He swallowed hard. "Yes. They kill. I tried to speak with them, or at least soothe them, but they were more afraid of me than I of them. I won't make that same mistake twice. The lion had a strange gleam in its eyes when it sniffed me. I don't think he will cower should we meet again."

"What will you do if you see it?"

Adam raised the stick in his hand and pounded it into the ground, as if to reassure her. "I'll deal with it as need be. Is the lamb still sleeping?"

She shook her head, troubled by the change in her husband. "Let me worry about your leg first." Sinking to her knees, she probed gentle fingers against his torn skin. "Oh, Adam. I fear dirt is inside this wound. Can you wash in the river while I find something to cover it with?"

Perhaps she was foolish to worry. After all, she had gotten her hands dirty in Eden and it had never hurt her. Why then, this sense of foreboding? But the wound was deep, and she could see the angry flesh, now stained red along the edges of the lacerated skin. She could see beyond the skin and leg hair, to a disturbing layer of flesh.

The cave spun as wooziness threatened to overtake her. Exhaling loudly, she forced herself to not quake at the sight. Again, she probed the wound until Adam winced.

Without him speaking a single word, she felt his will stiffening from the impatient look he shot her. Ah…perhaps he would not take her advice.

"Stop your fussing, Eve. I have work to do. We need food and more palm fronds to make a softer bed to lie on now that we sleep in this cursed cave." There it came, the acidic anger leaking from his voice.

"One dip in the river, that's all I'm suggesting," she said as she carefully brushed aside the dirt clinging to the hair of his legs. His skin felt unnaturally hot beneath her fingertips. "Your skin is turning red. Perhaps we don't need to fear only the animals. Maybe our new dangers are much smaller, but no less difficult." She softened her touch. "Please, Adam."

At last, he heeded her advice and yanked off his tunic just as she averted her gaze in time.

He was still beautiful to her. Achingly so. She longed to gaze upon him. Perhaps more than ever before.

With that long-legged stride, he marched toward the river and plunged into the rushing depths with a splash. When he surfaced, he slicked back his hair from his forehead. Biting the inside of her cheek, she fled the riverbank until at last she discovered a cluster of flowers growing out of the ground. Flowers at least provided a welcome distraction to the desire and frustration mounting within her.

Could she use flowers or herbs for healing, just as Father had used the Tree of Life?

She sniffed some of the pale white flowers and nibbled on the leaves of some, pausing only to spit out the bitter parts. One plant, a rod of golden flowers, grew in profusion next to the white flowers sprouting on thick green stems. She plucked both of them, perhaps guided more by a feeling.

Is this safe to use? How can I help Adam?

Father remained silent when she asked for help. Before, He had told her of the plants and their benefits. Whenever she had asked a question, He had immediately answered. Everything had a purpose, He had explained to her. A good purpose.

But now? She could only try on her own to discover that purpose.

Help me, Father. Please.

She grabbed as many of the flowers and stems as she could before returning to the cave. Adam had left the river. Dressed, he sat in the cave and carefully probed the broken leg of the lamb.

"I brought flowers," she said. "I wondered if I might use them to help you and the lamb. Something similar to the Tree of Life, perhaps?"

He didn't glance at her, his face now hardened as the rock surrounding them. Water dripped from his hair and dampened his leather tunic. "You brought flowers? Those will hardly feed us this evening."

She ignored the censure in his tone and placed the plants neatly on the wide leaf that once held the berries. If only she had a better solution to carry plants with the next time…

Regardless, she flushed when she glimpsed the sneer pulling at his lip.

With a grimace, Adam rose from the ground, reaching out to steady himself on the rock wall. "I need to gather a few things. Practical things that we can't do without."

"I'll help you," she offered quickly.

"No," he ground out between clenched teeth. "I don't know if the lion remains, and I want you here with the lamb." He shuffled out of the cave before she could form a coherent reply.

Your desire will be for your husband.

She had never argued with Adam in the garden. He had never limited nor dismissed her. A sharp retort filled her mind but only moments too late to challenge Adam. She ruthlessly pushed her angry thoughts aside.

The lamb's breathing had turned shallow, its meager chest barely fluttering with life. Any effort to feed the flowers to it resulted in failure. She sank back on her haunches, frustrated and feeling foolish for assuming the plants might help.

As she pinched one stem, a sticky sap leaked onto her fingertip.

Could she crush the plant and retrieve the juice from it? A large rock lay next to the leaf frond, which no longer held berries. She took the flowers and the rock. Pressing down on the rock, she gently crushed the entire plant. Flower, stem, delicate leaves, and pale roots, grinding the plants into a fragrant paste.

Meanwhile, she tried her best not to worry over Adam. Clearly, he was still angry with her.

The pulp stained her fingers green as she carefully fed the lamb. On closer inspection, it was older than the lambs she saw in the garden. Much older and larger. Would it survive without its mother's milk? How could she get it to drink water?

She stepped outside the cave, shielding her eyes against the harsh sun. The distance to the river was manageable, even if strewn with rocks and boulders. Perhaps she should carry the lamb. As carefully as she could, she lifted it into her arms, grunting at the weight. Down the treacherous hillside, her feet slid in the crumbling soil and slick stones. Somehow, she made it despite her arms straining with her additional burden.

At least the river ran clear. And the water felt icy. She drank from it and cupped her hand, bringing what she could to the poor creature, trickling the precious liquid into its mouth. Raising her head, she saw Adam approach the riverbank with a large palm frond rolled tightly in his arms. Dirt coated his hands and scraped knuckles. "I thought I told you to stay in that cave."

She winced at his tone, which seemed sharper than before. "The lamb would have died if it hadn't drunk or eaten. I fed it the flowers."

Her explanation brought a scowl to his lean features. He shoved the wrapped package, heavier than it first appeared, into her hands. "There are berries and a melon in that leaf. Be careful with it." He propped his fists on his hips, his lips pinched into a white line. Then, with a grunt, he reached down and picked up the lamb in his arms. "I'll carry the poor thing. I doubt she'll survive the night, even with something to drink."

Tenderly, Adam cradled the suffering creature, ignoring her as he trudged toward the cave. The scratch on his leg had reddened, engulfing his calf despite the dip into the river.

Silently, she followed him back into the cave.

CHAPTER EIGHT

For three days, the lamb struggled to live. For three days, Eve fed it a mash of flowers and grass and roots. She concocted different versions, making a paste for the marks on its skin, while Adam fretted over their survival. Meanwhile, the lion's hunting roar late at night frightened every living thing.

She no longer knew what it felt to have a full belly or to sleep without fear. Adam's temper festered the same as his aching leg.

"Let me treat your skin," she had begged the day before, as she had every other day. In his stubbornness, he had refused each time. Worse, he insisted on working from sunup to sundown. Here, unlike Eden, everything took so much more effort, reducing her husband to bitter tears.

"I've got to find a way to grow food, Eve. I've gathered everything I can find near our shelter. Either we move into the forest and keep gathering, or we stay here and make the cave our home."

"What if we kept wandering?" she offered as a suggestion. The idea of the sour-smelling cave replacing her cozy hill felt abhorrent.

He looked haunted when he stared at her. Bluish shadows curved beneath his eyes. "You haven't seen what I've seen out there in the wild. The animals are not the same. It's not just the lion who will kill us, but the wolves have now banded together and hunt as one. A deer with horns tried to gouge me yesterday. They're changing, Eve. Every single one of them. It's as though they are learning to shred each other to bits. I saw a porcupine with so many quills lash out at the wolf, sending the poor beast howling into the forest. I watched helplessly as a snake swallowed a small bird whole. Even the little bird fought back, with sharpened beak and talons. They are not my animals. Not the ones who nuzzled and licked my hands."

"Then let's stay at the cave." No longer did she try to encourage him to wander and explore.

He was too afraid to explore these days, preferring to keep things safe and contained in the areas he could control.

A growl escaped him. "We are going to have to hunt for animals to bring back to the cave. I don't want to do it, but I thought perhaps I might tame a few creatures for their milk. And if I can clear a patch of the forest and keep it safe from invaders, you and I can plant seeds together. All in one spot, with a decent harvest."

She tried to comfort him, but he brushed her aside, clearly preferring to be alone than speak with her. His new silence brought a fresh wave of fear. Being ignored was its own severe punishment, but the more she tried to engage Adam in conversation, the more he retreated.

Not knowing what else to do, she turned to the lamb and the plants, finding a small measure of comfort. Outside the cave, the wildflowers continued to sprout. She stepped outside of the cool darkness as much as she could, welcoming the faint rays of the sun on her shoulders and face. The tunic, even after a few days, was covered in dust and stains.

She sniffed herself and recoiled from her stench. A dip in the river would bring a welcome relief to the itching of her scalp and skin. Pausing beside the healing flowers, she snatched extra goldenrod. A sharp prick sent a well of red from her finger—just like Adam's leg. She sucked on her fingertip, the metallic hint unpleasant to her tongue. The plants had changed into something strange, just like the animals. Thorns pushed through stems and leaves. A new variety of green plants had popped up almost overnight, fed by the rising mist from the ground. They were choking out her goldenrod and herbal plants she used for healing.

She pulled out the recent growth, tossing it far from her treasured plants. Her patch of earth and flowers could be trained into something good. She was certain of it. When the flowers seeded, she would plant them as she saw fit.

After harvesting what she could, she made yet another paste for the lamb and her finger.

The lamb raised its head when she ducked into the cave. Its eyes appeared far brighter than the previous days. Thankfully, the violent red hue had faded from its wounds, even if it needed the brace for the leg. It pressed a wet nose against her hand, earning a cry of delight from her.

"You will rise again, little one. Show Adam how strong you are. Prove to him that the herbs work," she whispered. It bleated before snuggling against her for a nap.

If she wasn't so weary, she might have wept with relief.

Determined to let the lamb sleep in peace, she eyed the riverbank again. The sun had crested high, moving east. If she hurried, she might have a spare moment for a bath before he returned. Somehow, the dirt clung to her damp skin, unlike her time in Eden. And her body—the smells! She wiggled out of the leather covering and tucked it beneath one arm as she approached the muddy riverbank. The water felt shockingly cold to her feet. Forcing herself to walk farther into the water, she gasped as the air left her lungs. Regardless of the chill, it was a relief to wash her filthy hair and scalp. The last time she had bathed, she had swum with the turtles. The memory remained a bittersweet reminder of all she had lost.

Better to focus on the task at hand than to let her mind wander to Eden.

She scoured the stains on the tunic, using her jagged fingernails. A few stubborn marks remained on the leather despite her vigorous rubbing. With a sigh, she tossed the soggy garment onto the grass and immersed herself beneath the water. Fish darted away from her grasping fingers, flashing streaks of silver and green as they swam with the fast current.

Everything, except for the hurting lamb with a lame leg, ran away from her. Who knew loneliness could be so painful? How could she endure such a life?

Kicking her legs, she pushed to the surface, gasping for air. She held her breath and plunged a second time, feeling the current brush past her, tugging and strong. She tried to swim again, forcing herself to move harder and faster. Her muscles felt significantly weaker than when working in Eden. Lack of food? Or more evidence of the curse that God had promised?

Movement felt good, however, and a burst of energy coursed through her despite her hunger. When she emerged from the river, Adam stood by the riverbank, his arms filled with leafy greens and palm fronds.

His eyes widened with an unreadable expression when he saw her. Something appeared to hold him fast as he watched her snatch up her wet tunic and hold it up to cover her trembling form, her every impulse to jump back into the river and hide.

"Eve—" He swallowed hard before speaking again. "Eve, you needn't be afraid of me. I would never hurt you."

It wasn't fear she felt, but shame. Regardless, she bit the inside of her cheek. Her legs felt like stone beneath the weight of his heated gaze. Would he be angry that she had left the cave?

"Please," he said, his voice husky as he held out his hand for her to take. "I am your husband. If we are to be together, we can't hide from each other. I need you."

At those words, the tension seeped from her shoulders. Adam belonged to her. And she belonged to him. Just as her Father had intended. This was one gift that had not been completely lost or taken from her.

Morning light filtered through the cave. Eve slept by her husband's side. His even breathing brought a smile to her lips until she recalled his words the night before.

"I still want a child with you. If God commanded us to fill the earth, then at least in this, let us obey."

Yes, God had commanded them to fill the earth with children, but now she had pain to contend with, and that idea made her stomach roil. Yet how could she refuse Adam this request? He had certainly tried to provide a measure of comfort for her. Beneath them, a pile of palm fronds, leaves, and clumps of moss offered a respite to the rock floor. It wasn't Eden, but it was a marked improvement. Against the opposite wall of the cave, the lamb tried to rise on wobbly legs, the makeshift brace hindering its progress. However, that it wanted to stand was all the proof she needed.

Eve immediately sat up, unable to contain her excitement. "Adam, the lamb! The scratches are nearly healed, and the limb will be strong again."

He rubbed his bleary eyes and rose on one elbow. "What?"

She gestured toward the lamb. "Look for yourself." Dare she hope Adam would at least allow her to apply the same paste to his leg?

His mouth parted in wonder as he reached out to the small white bundle of wool. To her surprise, it pressed its nose against Adam's hand.

Adam's eyes watered as he captured the small lamb and brought it to his chest. He pressed his head against the wool, his chest rising and falling.

"Perhaps we can train the sheep to stay with us," she said, unable to keep from grinning.

"You healed her," Adam grudgingly admitted as he fingered the lamb's ears. Despite his gruffness, wetness shimmered from his eyes.

She shrugged, as he so often did. "Maybe we can try the same paste on your scratch."

Without a word, he stuck out his leg. Sucking in a surprised breath between her teeth, she snatched the last of her goldenrod and other herbs, using the rock to make a mash.

"You have a gift with plants, Eve." Her husband's quiet admiration made her heart stutter with pleasure. His hand stroked the lamb's head, which by now, closed its eyes.

"And you with animals." She busied herself with the paste, making it as smooth as she could. She really needed a firm surface to work on. Might she find a large flat rock to act as a base to grind her plants?

She bade him quickly wash again, which he did, and when he returned, she applied the paste onto the reddest portion of his skin.

"I had almost given up hope we could survive out here in this wilderness," he finally admitted after a long pause. "But you've made me reconsider. Between our gifts with plants and animals, we can have a new start."

He stroked the lamb's head. "A new start requires a new name, even for you, little lamb. I'll name you Mia."

Eve knew an opportunity when she saw one. "Let me help you outside. I can't stay any longer within these walls, or I'll lose myself. It's far too lonely, and I can't stand being alone with my thoughts. Adam, I need to see the greenery and feel the wind on my cheeks. I want to work the land with you and train the plants to become something we can use."

He was silent for a long moment, but when he released the lamb to her, she knew she had won.

"All right," he agreed. "But at the first sign of trouble, you'll return to where it is safe."

CHAPTER NINE

The wind brought much change in the many moons that followed. It howled against the cave, as frightening a sound as the lion that had returned to the riverbank to hunt, leaving tracks along the mud.

Adam often slept upright at the entrance of the cave, guarding her with a stout stick embedded with a jagged piece of rock—one of his newest inventions when he stumbled across a black shard so sharp, it cut into his fingers when he first reached for it. In the evenings, he clutched the weapon in his chapped hands, watching for any sign of predators. She missed him lying beside her, but with the lion stalking new prey, neither of them dared take any chances.

The previous day, they had discovered the fresh carcass of a deer in the forest, its gaunt form shredded from limb to limb. Bile rose in her throat at the sight, but Adam's features, now further bronzed from the sun, merely hardened. He walked around the carcass, kneeling down on the grass to study it. Flies swooped in and swarmed about the dead animal before Adam batted them away.

"I can save this hide," he noted coldly. "If we scrape it clean, we can lay it out to dry just like your fruits."

Sometimes it was difficult to recognize the fierce man who lived with her. Like the prickly thorns, Adam had changed into something she wasn't quite certain she always liked. Then again, just how much had she changed?

She struggled not to inhale through her nose, but breathing through her mouth was no better. Everything smelled so much stronger these days. The scent of grass and flowers was now sickly sweet. Pressing a fist against her mouth, she could hardly form a coherent answer.

"Eve?" he asked, arching an eyebrow when she bent over at the waist and threw up her morning meal of overripe melons. Much of the food rotted so quickly that she had taken to cutting it with the chiseled rock Adam had discovered. He had broken off a sliver with another blunt rock, the thin piece making it easier to slice the skin of the fruit and vegetables. Leaving those strips to dry beneath the sun also brought a new discovery. She could store food without it becoming covered in white mold—a blight that had made her violently ill the first time she tasted it.

That wasn't the only change. All she wanted to do was sleep. And though her limbs had grown leaner with the lack of consistent food, her stomach began to round. But she didn't have time to worry about such things, not with the lion back to hunt them or anything else that moved, and now, the impending coolness of the air, which slowed down the growth of her pitiful garden. Animals, birds, and insects loved her plants as well, stealing what they could. Starvation always loomed.

Leaves fell from the trees, signaling a change as temperatures plunged and rose. Meanwhile, the sky, once a rosy glow, churned with strange clouds Eve had never seen before. They towered, reaching to the height of the heavens, fierce and rumbling.

This day, Adam remained outside the cave, scraping the carcass of the fallen deer. He had pinned it with heavy rocks and had taken much of the afternoon cleaning it free of debris. He glanced up at the clouds, now the color of a mottled bruise. Meanwhile, the wind pushed against the grass, whipping her hair across her cheeks and cracked lips.

"Get back in the cave, Eve." Adam's harsh warning sent prickles scattering across her skin.

A roar deep within the trees made her hasten to obey. The lion had returned to the hunt for new prey. She scuttled across the boulders leading up to the cave, following the path worn smooth by her feet. Once inside the cave, she exhaled. The lamb, now the size of a sheep, greeted her with a timid bleat.

A rush of footsteps showed Adam had followed. He clutched his weapon and blocked the entrance of the cave with his large frame. A second roar, louder than the first, hinted that the lion might have caught wind of their scent.

Eve watched as her husband crouched low, holding out his weapon outward. A flash of tawny fur outside the cave and Adam's hiss brought a fresh stab of fear. Her husband could not withstand an attack a second time. The teeth and claws alone of such a monster would render him like the slain deer.

Dare she call on God? His silence had been the most painful cost of all.

She bowed her head and reached out to her Father with her mind. *Please help. Please do not abandon us. We need You, Father.*

The sky answered in a rumble and a crackle far louder than the lion. The very sound shook the cave. A flash of white arced across the sky, flinging tendrils of light into the black clouds. It sizzled and shot downward, near the lion pacing outside the cave, and stabbed into the ground. The resulting boom that followed sent her face down to the pebble-strewn floor.

When she dared to raise her head, Adam had already left the cave with his weapon. He stood next to the flames licking the dry grass. For a moment, he appeared immobile, his gaze trapped by the orange flare that resembled the fire rippling down the length of the angelic sword guarding Eden.

Then, to her shock, he jogged toward the forest. The lion was nowhere to be found, and when Adam returned, he carried a small bundle of sticks. Jabbing them into the fire, he waited long enough for the branches to glow red. Instead of blowing out the fire, the wind merely fed the flames. Adam loped toward her while grasping the burning bundles. He ducked into the shadowed cave, his stern features highlighted by the fire.

She scuttled backward on the ground, intending to give herself as much room as possible from that dreadful light.

Coughing, he placed the bundle on the rock floor.

"I don't think the fire will hurt you. Not if you don't touch it."

"I'm not moving from this spot," she rasped. The image of the fiery sword blocking her from Eden renewed a fresh terror.

Adam held his hand over the dancing flames, his mouth quirking to one side. "It's warm, Eve. See? I'm fine." His hand lowered as a now rare mischievous twinkle entered his eyes. His humor evaporated, and he yanked it back with a yelp. "Perhaps that was *too* close."

Was the fire God's answer to her silent pleas? Was Father listening, after all?

"I prayed to Father, begging Him to deliver us from that lion," she admitted. "I had feared He had completely abandoned us."

Adam's expression flickered as he studied the growing fire and the dancing smoke. "I feared the same." He said no more, staring into the dying flames as the red embers floated higher, caught in the now gentle breeze.

Would Father send a deliverer as He had promised? She wrapped her arms around her waist. Would He still watch over her and direct her path? Or was she too far removed from Him to recover their gutted relationship?

After fire made quick work of the dried branches, Adam left to gather more. Meanwhile, she crept closer to the flames. The warmth felt rather nice, and truthfully, her body ached terribly these past several days. Especially her stomach. Her appetite had fled, leaving her feeling sickly. Perhaps not wanting to eat was a respite from the constant hunger. She lay down on the palms and rushes, cradling her belly. A flutter answered in her abdomen, as gentle as butterfly wings.

She closed her eyes. When she opened them, Adam sat next to her. He had gathered quite a supply of wood, and the wind had died down, leaving only the sound of twigs and branches cracking and popping. Smoke billowed from the flames, but the open cave offered an escape. A pleasant light flickered across the cave walls, highlighting every undulating curve and stretch of granite. But Adam wasn't looking at the cave. He was looking at her. Studying her.

His brows pinched together as he placed his hand on the curve of her stomach. She glanced down, her tunic stretched tighter than she had remembered. His next words jolted her out of her sleepiness.

"Eve, I think you are going to have a baby."

CHAPTER TEN

If she thought having a child would please Adam and draw him closer to her, she was only partially right. Pleased he was. But the idea of providing for three threw him into a frenzy of endless activity.

His mind never seemed to stop planning on how to improve their life. Together, they discovered dried animal dung burned slower and smoked less than the branches. Moreover, it chased away the pesky mosquitos that left welts all over her arms and legs. Wet branches as fuel were useless, tainting everything with the stench of smoke.

She collected as much of the dung as she could and stored it in the driest portion of the cave. As long as the fire kept burning, they would have some small measure of comfort. Meanwhile, Adam used fire to reshape the land, burning away the dead plants and trees. Sometimes, it ran away from him, encroaching into the forest and destroying everything in its path.

The resulting orange glow covering the landscape had frightened her. When the fire finally subsided, the heat and the flames turned everything to gray ash with flakes of debris floating in the air. A world of ruin before beginning afresh.

The idea made her want to grind her teeth together.

Following one such devastating fire, she discovered the charred remains of other deer when they emerged from the safety of their cave. A single fox, its fur singed along the brown tail, paused over the charred remains, scavenging what it could. It snarled once in warning and ran away when Adam approached the scorched ground. He used his staff to etch a line into the blackened earth, now devoid of brush and tangled ferns.

"We can plant seeds here and tend to a field."

"But what about the other animals who steal daily from my garden?" she asked. Now that the wildlife had discovered her patch of greenery, she had to scrounge for half-eaten leftovers. Only the squash and underground vegetables survived, and barely at that, most of the plants decimated with worms or mold.

"I'll build a border around it, just like the one in Eden. We'll use it to keep everything out."

He knelt down on the ground and poked into the carcass, removing bones and whatever else he could from the remains. Everything became an instrument in his hands. She knew later he would devise something of use with the bones. Over the past moons, she had collected a variety of sharpened tools for scraping the dead hides of animals or digging holes into the ground to plant seeds.

"I've been thinking," Adam began, almost halting, after he made a pile on the ground of the items he would claim later.

"Yes?" she asked after a long pause. It was becoming increasingly rare for him to talk, or to have the time to listen to her chat.

"I've been thinking about what God what said in the garden—about sending a deliverer, one the serpent will try to bruise."

He eyed her blossoming stomach. Instinctively, she placed her hand on top of her round belly.

"Eve, I want to please Him again. I don't want to remain separate from God anymore. I want to offer a sacrifice. An animal. Not a sickly one."

She gasped at the idea. "Why, Adam?"

He rose from the ground, clenching his fists at his sides. "Do you remember what God did after we ate the fruit?"

The memory had been branded into her mind. How could she forget? "Father killed two deer."

Adam nodded. "An animal sacrifice. There is a cost for sin, and as God noted, we can no longer abide with Him in our current state. We need to offer a sacrifice if we are to please Him."

"Why not offer the fruits and vegetables?" she protested. Already the idea of routinely killing animals on behalf of her sin made her recoil.

"Did He kill squash and clothe us with melons? No, He shed blood on our behalf, draping us with these garments. Our disobedience can't be covered with something so trite as purple carrots. I want to continue what He began, Eve. We will offer sacrifice with each new moon. And I want us to rest again on every seventh day—just as we did in the garden. We will obey Him as best we can."

She stiffened at the idea of her plants considered as trite and unworthy to be offered to God. "Why now, Adam? It's been many moons since we've done such things."

He brushed aside a tangled lock of hair, now long enough to graze his shoulder blades. "Because I don't want my child to be separated from God the way we are. If you and I can regain what we have lost, then I want to do it. I need to try to please Him again."

Could Adam bridge the gap? Father had warned that sin would separate them from Him and bring death. Could Adam somehow earn his way back to God? Was it as simple as trying to follow Father's commands and working to become a better person?

"What will you sacrifice?" she finally dared to ask.

His gaze didn't waver when he turned to regard her. "A lamb."

An unintelligible sound escaped her lips when she thought of their rescued lamb, now full grown. Mia felt like family, especially considering the aloofness of the other animals.

"Not our sheep in the cave. I found some lambs roaming wild in a herd, to the east of us."

She didn't dare argue with Adam. If she did, he would retreat for days, leaving her in total silence. But truthfully, the idea of killing an innocent creature to cover her sins brought only pain.

Before Adam built the stone wall around the fields, he layered a column of stones with mud, creating a platform waist-high. She hated the sight of it. Why must he build a spot for sacrifices? It was a constant reminder of all that she had done, and all the ways she had failed and would continue to fail.

When he left one day, intending to bring back a lamb for sacrifice, she hid herself in the shadowed cave. All of this was her fault. If only she hadn't picked the fruit. If only she had been content with her life before risking everything for one silly, measly bite.

Regardless, Adam could not be reasoned with in this new quest of killing.

"I must sacrifice or our crops will fail," he had informed her before leaving. She waited in the cave, using a sharpened needle of bone and strips of hide to sew satchels for gathering the harvest. At her feet, the attempts of weaving lay ignored. For days, she had tried to weave strips of leather and dried reeds into something that might form a container to store the coming harvest. Adam feared the changes in the weather. He also feared that should a herd of animals trample through the food supply, it would leave them truly destitute. Better to dry and store what food she could for the coming seasons. Or surely death would come, slow and filled with hunger.

The sun had crossed the sky when he returned to the cave with a wild lamb tied at the legs with sturdy vines. The frightened creature remained pinned beneath his arms. How strange to see such a sight. She had grown used to seeing only tenderness from him when he worked in Eden.

"I wish you wouldn't hurt the poor lamb," she said between clenched teeth as she lay aside her satchel. "It's done nothing wrong to deserve such treatment."

"Come," he said, ignoring her challenge. Inwardly, she berated him as she followed his retreating form out of the cave and into the last of the sunset. At least he didn't insist she help. Instead, he lay the animal on top of the platform.

Then, with his sharpened bone honed to a lethal point, he stabbed the creature with one fell swoop, before carving out the best portions of the lamb, including the fat, and placing the remains onto the altar to be consumed with fire.

A brutal action to her way of thinking.

But her husband's voice broke, belying the violence of the gesture. "God, please take this offering on behalf of Eve and me. Forgive us for our sins."

She covered her hand with her mouth, wanting nothing more than to protest his declaration. She wanted nothing to do with this. But to her shock, Adam's shoulders shook as if he silently sobbed.

He continued speaking out loud, oblivious to the protest building inside her. "I cannot hear You, Father. But I vow with everything in me that my family and I will serve You. Do not abandon us in our need."

When the wind dipped in temperature and the birds found refuge elsewhere for the season as marked by the constellations in the sky, Eve forced herself to work alongside Adam. She carried the larger rocks from the riverbed, helping him build a wall around the field. It was an impressive wall, nearly as high as her waist. Adam slathered a clay-like mud between each flat rock, and when the clay dried, the structure held.

She tried to forget the sacrifice in her mind and the image of blood dripping down the sides of the makeshift altar, but it wasn't easy. Father had warned death was the cost. And though life surrounded her, death also lurked in the rushing current of the river, in the rotting foliage of the forest floor, and wherever predators stalked in the hollows and thickets.

Forcing herself to pay attention to the task at hand, she banished the troubling thoughts from her head as Adam smeared a gray mud across one rock with his fingers.

She bent down, her round belly an impediment. Still, she persisted as she reached for more stones. With a groan, she lifted the nearest rock, when a pain rippled through her abdomen.

She dropped it with a thud and braced herself against the wall.

"Eve"—he glanced at her with a frown—"what is wrong?"

Adam had helped plenty of animals give birth in Eden but never with her. Father's warning shuddered through her as she splayed her fingers across her belly.

"I will make your pains in childbearing very severe; with painful labor you will give birth to children."

"It's nothing," she wheezed in between muscle spasms. After several deep breaths, the pain evaporated.

He stared at her, his green eyes round with alarm.

"I'm not as fragile as you assume. We will build this wall before our child arrives. Then we won't have to worry about our food supply."

Adam looked unconvinced, even when she bent over a second time and hoisted a large rock, offering it to him to take.

He quickly snatched it and placed it on the fresh layer of mud. "I'll do it myself. I won't have you injured."

"But you can't tend to the crops and the weeding and the building all by yourself. There isn't enough sunlight during the day. Let me help you. Between the two of us, we'll have things finished much sooner."

He opened his mouth as if to argue with her and then snapped his jaw shut. "If you hurt again, you must promise me you'll rest."

"Of course," she agreed, but it wasn't exactly the truth. Retreating into the dismal cave simply wasn't an option for her.

In the moons that followed, she finished the wall with Adam, her desire to see a task accomplished overriding everything else. Other triumphs occurred. She conquered the reeds, shaping and weaving them into a simple platter. Then she made a bowl shape so that the produce wouldn't tumble over the sides. The weaving of reeds brought so many possibilities to consider in making her life easier. A tuft of sheep wool, retrieved from the thicket, waited beside the latest basket. When she had tugged at it, the threads separated, each strand full of promise.

Adam had discovered that milk from the goats abated the hunger. One day, he stumbled into a beehive and brought home a dripping comb of honey for her to savor, his grin returning despite a swollen bee sting marring his wrist.

A change of season occurred with new life budding beneath the crumbling soil. More babies were born to the deer and the sheep and the wolves. Birds laid speckled eggs in carefully constructed nests high in the trees or hidden among the rocks, signaling renewal. The babe within her grew and grew. Surely her child would appear at any moment. Excitement flared within her at the idea of holding her child.

Adam hardly rested. Nor could she, even with an extra layer of palm fronds to cushion her burgeoning form. He lay beside her as a faint dawn lightened the sky. Placing a warm hand on her belly, he leaned in to snuggle her in a rare moment. Beneath the weight of his fingers, the baby kicked hard.

"He's restless and ready to get out," Adam remarked with a hint of awe.

She smiled when her husband didn't move away. If only she could keep Adam closer to her. Would a son draw them together? By now, her skin had stretched smooth, rippling with faint white lines. She resembled a ripe melon more than anything else, and her gait reminded her of the elephants that plodded along the riverbank.

"Hopefully, it won't be long before our baby makes his appearance."

Adam sighed and sat up from the mat. He reached for his staff and rose.

"Aren't you going to eat anything this morning?"

"No," he said gruffly. "I'm not that hungry." As if to expose the lie, his belly rumbled loudly. As of late, he avoided eating a second meal, leaving the meager portions only for her.

"Where are you going today?" she asked, fearing the answer.

"I'm going to find extra sheep to keep company with Mia. Maybe another hen or two so we have extra eggs to eat. I'll herd them into the walled-off portion."

"I'll join you." The baby in her womb kicked again, stealing the rest of her protest. She didn't like eating the raw eggs—something Adam had tried previously when he had been nearly fainting with hunger.

"Not today, Eve. You can barely walk as it is. You'll only slow things down if you try to help."

His harsh answer hurt more than the tiny legs wiggling with impatience inside her.

She consoled herself that at least she had Mia for company. Now thoroughly tamed, Mia kept close to the cave. But truthfully, Eve wanted nothing more than to be outside among the green leaves and fragrant wildflowers. If Adam would let her, she would sleep outdoors, beneath the stars, as she once had.

Snatching his spear, he abandoned her to another long day in the cave, where she was forced to confront her turbulent thoughts. Tears welled in her eyes as she snatched strips of long grass, grape vines, and blackberry canes and looped them together to form yet another platter.

The sprouting of thorns lining the plants pricked her fingers, forcing her to strip the canes with her rocks. She had learned to place the reeds in a horizontal and then vertical positioning, using one vine to wrap around the cross formation. Then she twisted and separated the vines until a clumsy circle formed. From there, she interlaced the grass strips, canes, and vines. The work was painstaking and mind-numbing. But the end results were rather satisfying. Even Adam approved of the idea.

She quickly used the last of the reeds, left with a half-finished platter. Could she collect more in the forest nearby? Taking the obsidian rock chiseled to a fine point, she snatched her leather satchel. The walk felt so good for her sore back. But by the time she reached the forest, a familiar stabbing pain slowed her steps.

She ignored it, focusing on slicing the nearest vines and sliding the pieces into her satchel. A shaky breath escaped her as she fingered a variety of leaves, some fuzzy, some smooth and thick, and others fragile. The greenery brought a soothing to her spirit. With no lion in sight, she continued working, taking what stems she could find.

Adam was far too worried about her.

"I won't remain cooped up in the cave for the rest of my life. *I won't do it,*" she muttered out loud. But the next wave of pain nearly forced her to her knees.

Dropping the satchel, she could only clutch her belly as the muscles within her contracted over and over again.

CHAPTER ELEVEN

Eve hobbled along the path, her home hidden by the thick foliage. By the time she saw the welcome sight of the river, a foul water mysteriously gushed between her legs. With a low moan, she reached out to brace herself against a nearby trunk.

The warning echoed again in her mind. *"I will make your pains in childbearing very severe."*

She thought she knew what pain was, until now. Stubbed toes, a wasp sting, scratches from thorns, the cold of the river, and a stomach throbbing with hunger. But none of them compared to the waves of agony riding through her, tearing her apart from within.

A harsh cry rent through her as she slowly slid to the ground. She lost track of time as she squatted on the grass, rocking back and forth with each contraction. A rattle through the sickly sweet-smelling weeds sent a fresh quiver of alarm as a snake slithered toward her, its black tongue flickering in and out. Green and yellow stripes marked its undulating body.

"I will put enmity between you and the woman, and between your offspring and hers; he will crush your head, and you will strike his heel."

This serpent was not the silver-tongued enemy from the garden, but she scrabbled nonetheless from it, her movements clumsy and far too slow to put much space between the two of them. Panic bubbled up inside her as she locked her gaze with its beady eyes. With a hiss, it rose and swayed as if to dart forward and attack her. She screamed just as a rock flew and struck the snake, sending it rearing back into the long grass.

She was floating above the ground. Dimly, she realized Adam was carrying her. He ducked into the cave, keeping a tight grip on her. Carefully, he laid her on the mat of reeds and palm leaves. To her immense relief, he didn't chide her for leaving the shelter of the cave.

"Eve, speak to me." He ran his hands gently over her body, his expression alarmed.

Another contraction stole her breath. She nearly sobbed when she could finally speak. "I saw a serpent. It tried to attack me. Adam, the baby, he's coming."

He grasped her feet, carefully inspecting her calves as well. "I see no bite. It's gone now, Eve. You are safe. It can't hurt you."

As the sun fled into the horizon, Adam made certain the fire crackled, illuminating the rugged cave walls with a fiery glow. Eve's labor began in earnest. She gave in to the pain, pushing with all of her might to find some alleviation, but the baby would not come. Pacing no longer helped. Crouching, with Adam's' support, she braced herself. Adam placed careful fingers on her stomach, searching where the child might lie.

He was infinitely tender as he looped his arms around her. "Tell me what I must do, Eve. How can I help?"

She had no answer for him as she strained with all her might, pushing with every muscle, willing her baby to move. Why wouldn't her child come into the world? Sweat dripped down her back and forehead, and her skin felt as though she were on fire.

Push and push and push. The rhythm of pain intensified until there was no more relief between the squeezing of her abdomen. A scream ripped from her, full-throated and like the roar of the lion that had haunted their camp.

Adam's brows lowered as he shifted beside her, rubbing her back with a renewed vigor. "What can I do? There must be something I can do to ease this pain."

But there was nothing he could do. When she bit down on her lip, he snatched a piece of wood and slipped into her mouth when she finally opened it to breathe again.

"Eve..." His voice lowered to a moan as he touched her swollen bottom lip.

Was this the end for her? Before long, she felt herself slipping away, carried on a black river that threatened to swallow her whole. It was all too easy to succumb to that great river and give up any last claim to life.

Father, she reached out with her mind, *I haven't any more strength*. Her child would die with her. She would not see the deliverer come, for death claimed all in the end. Grief brought a despair that she hadn't the strength to fight anymore.

Beside her, Adam wept. "Eve, don't leave me!"

She felt him wrap his arms around her, while his tears fell onto her cheeks and slid down her neck.

Another groan ripped free from him as he rested his head against hers. "I can't lose her, Father. Please don't take her and my son from me. Please, have mercy."

The ringing in her ears became a roar as she struggled to breathe.

God had promised her He would send a deliverer through her seed. She hadn't believed Him the first time, regarding the tree. Shouldn't she trust His word—that He would fulfill exactly as He promised?

Yet the pain inside her screamed that her situation was hopeless. Impossible. Death waited to drag her into the last horizon, one of terror and separation.

She wanted to believe God would keep His promise. She had to believe.

With a whimper, she pushed one last time, helpless against the contractions pulling at her as the baby descended. Adam released his hold on her, his hands outstretched to catch their child. As the world faded, she heard Adam's triumphant cry.

"I see him, Eve! Praise God, our son is born!"

Her son's wail as he choked for air brought a wave of relief to Eve. Her baby. Her darling baby boy, his skin once bluish and frightening, now pinked as he flailed his fists, each limb coated in a strange white film, and bawled again.

A strange feeling, perhaps a result of the labor, coursed through her as she watched Adam hold his son to his chest.

Her husband glanced at her, his gaze finally warm. "He's a fighter, our child, like the lion that tussled with the wolf. I cannot believe how perfect he is. Five fingers and five toes on each limb. Everything is so tiny and wonderful."

Adam lowered his head closer to his son's intense gaze. "I think he has blue eyes. The color of the sky near evening." He kissed his son on the cheek, the reward being a second wail.

Her baby waved his frail arms, his features awash in red. Adam approached her, but she noticed a dangling cord from her child's stomach.

"Adam! What is that thing attached to our child?" She couldn't keep the horror from her voice.

He fingered the slippery appendage with his free hand before wrinkling his nose. "I've seen this same sac with the animals. Our son has been born with a cord attached to his belly. It's as though God placed our child inside a miraculous satchel inside of you. You released it not long after the birth. I wonder if I should cut the cord?"

She sounded indignant despite her exhaustion. "You must cut it! Cain can't have a string attached to him when he grows up to be a man."

Adam flashed her a grin, revealing a flash of white teeth. "I agree."

Then he paused. "You want to call him Cain?"

She wanted to name their child. "With the help of the Lord, I have brought forth a man. Father kept His promise, Adam. He promised us a deliverer, and I believe Cain will be that man who will save us. It is the perfect name for a perfect son."

Adam didn't answer her bold claim as he carefully laid Cain onto her breast. Her son latched onto her breast and suckled. The noisy sounds filled the cave, and she smiled even though the labor had proven far more draining and traumatic than she could have imagined.

"I thought you were dying," Adam said gruffly as he brushed aside her damp hair from her forehead. His fingers trembled against her skin, tracing a path to the shell of her ear. "Never frighten me like that again."

How could she make such a promise? Worse, she feared that his urge to protect her would keep her trapped forever inside the damp place they now called home. Her spirit balked at such a life, forced into a safety that brought no joy or purpose.

He reached for a chip of the obsidian rock, one with an edge so sharp that it sliced through an animal's hide as easily as through a palm frond. Once her baby finished eating, his eyes closed in sleep and his cheeks flushed, she let Adam take her baby.

Inhaling sharply, Adam placed their son beside her. "Forgive me, little one. I hope this won't hurt."

With a swift motion, he sliced the cord attached to Cain. Cain's eyes fluttered opened and his answering wail at being wakened pierced the stillness. Wincing, Adam studied the boy's slight form before knotting the rest of the cord.

"He has a knot," Eve said as she reached for her son again and placed him against her body. In response, Cain closed his eyes, his rosebud mouth making sucking motions against her skin.

She continued to marvel over her child. Her stomach was perfectly smooth, as was Adam's. No evidence of a knot or any marring. Would her son resent such a mark when he was old enough to understand? She closed her eyes, ready to sleep, when Adam settled down beside her. Carefully, he laid his arm about her waist, drawing close enough to rest his head against hers. He kept his grip deliberately light, yet the safety of him earned a sigh from her.

Her pulse slowed with each of her husband's deep breaths as he nuzzled her neck as if to draw comfort from her. Her heart nearly burst with happiness despite the prior suffering. She marveled at her small family. If only this moment, and Adam's attention, would last. For now, she would savor what she had been given.

In a cocoon of warmth and peace, she finally drifted to sleep.

CHAPTER TWELVE

Several seasons later

"Mama, please, can I have another apple?"

Eve glanced at her son, who, by now, was nearly as high as her waist. Cain blinked at her, his gaze completely innocent. He rubbed his black hair with a filthy hand that had likely traced pictures of the animals into the silt of the riverbank. But, truthfully, it was the third apple he had sneaked this morning when he thought no one was looking. He had taken each of them without asking her permission.

She bit the inside of her cheek to quell a quick retort. "How many apples have you eaten, Cain?"

His eyes, no longer blue, glowed hazel in the sunlight. They widened at her challenge. He rubbed his lean arms. "I'm not sure. I'm so hungry, Mama. Father says I could eat one more."

She squinted against the bright light, holding her hand to shield her eyes, and glanced toward where Adam worked. A glimpse of his strong form bending, lifting, smoothing more mud on the rock wall as he repaired the enclosure, which protected grains, squash, and melons for the upcoming harvest, showed he had stayed for most of the morning. Had Cain run to Adam earlier and asked permission?

She highly doubted it. Adam maintained strict rules about the food storage, which had yet again grown perilously low these days.

The sun had reached the midday point. Her husband would want food soon. She ducked inside the cave, the walls further blackened with smoke over the past many moons.

A heavy sigh escaped her. The filthy cave felt like a great yawning hole, determined to suck her into its inky depths. Mia and the other sheep lived inside during the evening, safe from the wolves and the venomous snakes which slithered through the grass. But it would never compare to her fragrant hill in Eden. Too many competing smells demanded her attention: dung, sweat, and soot. None of them she liked.

She brushed aside a stray lock of hair as she gathered additional supplies. "Come, Cain. I've finished my chores for the morning. Surely your father could use our help."

The morning had sped all too quickly as she inspected the new herbal plants blossoming from small wicker baskets. She had created a medicinal patch, placing the baskets onto a ledge jutting outward from the cave rock wall facing the sun. With the next full moon, once Adam finished his work, she planned to transplant her tiny plants into the larger enclosed field.

Her son groaned out loud.

"Why don't we bring Father apples? He must be hungry, considering all the hard work he has done this morning."

Cain pushed out his lower lip. "I don't want to go. Father will make me pull out the weeds, and I don't want to do it."

She clucked her tongue, her patience fading with her son's attitude. "We all work, Cain. You know we need to grow and harvest the food before we eat it."

It was Adam's favorite explanation whenever she or Cain questioned the never-ending turmoil of tending the fields and the livestock. If Adam wasn't tending the small field, he was dreaming of what improvements he would attempt next. The only improvement she wished was to leave the cave and sleep beneath the stars, but Adam wouldn't hear of it. Not after the first seasons with the ravenous lion.

In fact, it seemed he cared more for his growing livestock, which now comprised sixty sheep, twenty goats, fifteen hens, and a cocky rooster who crowed at every dawn. The sheep and goats provided the milk, skins, and wool, which he sheared with his obsidian blades. The hens provided plenty of eggs, which Adam and Cain guzzled, slurping the yellow yolk inside. She couldn't muster the appetite to do the same. A cracked egg had led to the discovery of the yolk inside, and since Adam explored and tasted what he could, just as she often did, it proved an additional meal source.

Adam's only concession was to rest on the seventh day. She was grateful for at least that rest, but the long days and nights wrestling with the garden and livestock had proven challenging. Especially since a group of foxes had scattered the hens, eating what they could while trampling and crushing the remaining eggs.

She grabbed her satchel and slipped in the last of the apples as a treat. Three sickly options, including one brown and mushy on the bottom. She would save that fruit for herself. The past season had been unusually wet, the mist rising and watering the ground likely due to water running underground, as Adam had found deep and secret rivers in the lower regions of the cave. But a new rot had decimated more than half of the plantings. Mold. Blight. Worms. Insects and caterpillars. Birds. Anything that moved or preyed upon their fields. Something constantly besieged her garden with new threats.

No wonder Adam wrestled with the ground, as if he could beat it into submission and reclaim the bit of the paradise he had once savored. But they had lost Eden forever. With every waxing moon they knew each day might be their last in this wild world.

Outside the meadow, beyond the untamed meadows and the river, she witnessed far too many animals hunting each other for food. Elephants and other creatures bellowed their rage during the midnight hour. In response to the overwhelming danger, the male deer and antelope grew grotesque horns. The lion's teeth sharpened into formidable tools so long as to protrude over lips. Everything had a defense or a weapon, including the wasp, which flashed its stinger if she startled it near a flower. Every new moon, the weeds grew taller and stronger, hiding her precious plants from the much-needed sunlight.

The curse permeated everything, much like the morning fog rolling over the plains and river.

She glanced at Cain, every hope that he would deliver her pinned on his narrow shoulders.

"Mama? Can I have that apple?" He tugged at her bag, his small hand already dipping into the interior, before pulling out a fruit.

"Wait, Cain," she murmured. "Let's eat with your father."

She knew what it felt to be impatient, to want so much more in the moment. Perhaps her patience with Cain would bring him to a better understanding. So she curbed her tongue and led her son out of the cave.

As they made their way down the beaten path worn flat by their feet, Cain chatted happily with her. He reached with his hand, snatching hers to squeeze tightly. Any chiding she felt compelled to give melted away with that winsome smile of his. How beautiful, her son. He resembled her more and more as the days passed, with his chin pointed and his cheekbones high.

"I want to explore the meadow, but Father says I can't go without him. And he never has time to explore or wander."

"Your father has many cares. Be patient with him, Cain. He cares very much for you and me."

Cain merely glowered, mimicking his father at the moment, but he didn't protest as he normally did.

Our son is a fighter, like the lioness who hunts at night," Adam had said about Cain.

Didn't she know it, daily matching her will against her son's?

She banished the troubling thought as she approached Adam. Her husband straightened when he saw her, his expression grim. His chin was smeared with a reddish clay, and his fingers remained equally stained. He wore a new leather skirt, leaving his chest bare and tanned.

Raising her satchel, she spoke, "I brought a few apples. Why don't you take a small rest and sit down and enjoy a bite to eat?"

He blew out a harsh breath, stirring his long hair, which by now had fallen over his eyes and spilled down onto his back, rivaling her hair's length. "I don't have time to rest. The old mud between the rocks dissolved, and the eastern section of the wall is about to collapse. If I don't fix it, our fields will be exposed to the wildlife yet again. We've already lost most of our food supply. I don't know how we'll make it in the season to come."

It was true. The other night, she had run her fingers over her ribs, now jutting outward beneath her skin. Adam's chest and arms had thinned, but most painful of all was Cain's spindly form. She and Adam gave most of the food to their only child to combat the gnawing hunger.

Never would she have imagined how painful hunger could feel.

She surveyed the damaged section, noting how the stones buckled outward, as if a giant hand had pushed them into that position. "Just a moment of rest to spend with your family. I'm not asking for the rest of the day."

Adam scowled when he noticed Cain. "Where have you been? I told you to bring fresh clay in that basket long ago."

She felt Cain's small fingers reach for her hand. His hazel eyes widened even more with Adam's strident tone.

Squaring her shoulders, she faced her husband. "Cain was hungry. He said you told him he could have another apple."

Her answer, blurted out before she could consider the ramifications, made her husband straighten to his full height, which was considerable. Her son shrank beside her.

He glowered at both of them. "Cain, you disobeyed me. You ran away when I needed your help the most. How can I complete this wall without your help?"

"I'll help," Eve cut in quickly. "I've finished tending to my herbs. Tell me what you need me to do."

Over the past moons, Adam increasingly relied on her gardening and medicinal herbs. As long as she didn't wander too far from their settlement, she gathered what she could. Her pastes and dried leaves had brought relief for toothaches, headaches, scratches, and burns. No longer did Adam dismiss her concoctions as useless.

Adam sighed as he braced himself against the stone wall that remained secure. "I want my son to learn how to work. There's far too much to do than for him to muck around the riverbank chasing butterflies."

She flinched at the accusation in his voice. The previous day of rest, she had taken Cain to that very riverbank and chased the butterflies dancing in the air. Later, she and Cain had wandered as far as they could, following the lightning bugs that glimmered at twilight. Cain had tried to capture one to bring it back to the cave. A wonderful memory.

She leaned in, whispering so that Cain wouldn't overhear. "You push our son to his breaking limit. He's just a child, no different from the lambs that frolic in the meadow. Is Cain not to enjoy his childhood and have a morning or afternoon of play?"

Adam pinched his lips together into a white line. "I'm not against playing or rest. But how can you coddle him so? Don't you see that he lied about the apple? He also disobeyed a direct command from me—his own father. Why do you let him get away with so much? You will ruin him."

Anger, along with a prick of guilt, coursed through her as she stared back at him. Did she coddle Cain? Surely not. If only Adam had showed her understanding, and her Father too. Cain was so much like her, it was as if she could almost read the thoughts tumbling through his inquisitive mind. He was incredibly curious and bright, wanting to explore the vast horizons beyond their cave and walled fields—apparently a character flaw in the eyes of Adam.

"If you showed your son a touch of compassion, he might be more willing to work by your side. Instead, you constantly glower and bark commands every time he or I make a mistake. We can't work hard enough for you. We can't enjoy life because of you—"

Perhaps those words were unfair, but Adam's accusations unleashed something inside of her, something hot and acrid.

"Me?" he squawked, no longer attempting to hide his rising volume. He slapped the wall, sending the top stone tumbling over the side. "*Me?* How dare you accuse me of not enjoying life, Woman! Who gave me the forbidden fruit to eat in the first place?"

She pressed a shaking hand against her chest. "You could have stopped me from eating that fruit. The serpent lied, but you held your tongue. Were you not aware of his lies?"

Adam reared back from her accusation, his features pale. "I see perfectly how this is to be between us. You view me as a failure. Both as a man and as a father."

Cain's enormous eyes welled with tears as he dashed in between Eve and Adam. One tear escaped, leaving a silver track down a filthy cheek. "Why do you both always fight? Why must you be so mean to each other? I don't want to live here anymore with either of you." He spun on his heel and raced into the forest before she could grab his arm.

"He will come back," she whispered, more to comfort herself. "Cain always comes back to us."

Adam grunted as he braced his palms on the strongest portion of the wall and vaulted over the side. She watched as he jogged into the woods, determined to catch Cain. A startled howl soon echoed through the forest. Wincing, she folded her arms across her chest just as Adam returned with a squirming bundle pinned beneath one arm.

He paused long enough to let their son slide free. "I'll spank you again if you ever disrespect me with lies. We don't sneak fruit. You will ask your mother's permission before you ever take from her again."

"It's fine, really, Adam," Eve protested. "Please don't be mad at Cain. Please don't hurt him."

A protest too late by the look of things.

She palmed the back of her neck, a fresh ache intensifying, moving upward to her temples. The stress between them brought a host of physical ailments, rendering her almost useless, especially when the headaches blossomed until she saw lights spinning. Only then did she crave the quiet hush of the cave and the darkness it brought.

Cain's cheeks were stained with tears as he rubbed his bottom where Adam's hand had likely collided.

Adam turned toward her, his heated expression cooling. "We will hurt him later, Eve, if we let him get away with such things."

Suddenly, she no longer wanted to spend time with Adam. The apples and newly washed vegetables in her satchel felt too heavy to carry. Unable to speak, she held out her hand for Cain to take as she unslung the leather bag and let it fall to the ground.

CHAPTER THIRTEEN

"Did I transplant the orchid right, Mama?"

Eve glanced at her ten-year-old son, who held a basket with a lush purple blossom unfurling with vibrant green leaves. She poked into the soil with a finger, pleased to discover it was neither too dry nor too wet. Her basket design allowed for the excess water to drip, leaving the roots of the plant free to breathe.

"It's perfect. You have a gift with plants."

Cain flashed her a sweet grin as he carried the basket, placing it beside the newly walled garden Adam had created for her. "Just like you."

She grinned in return, warming at the compliment. The connection with her son was a bittersweet one. The more Cain grew these past moons, his lanky form stretching, the more Adam demanded a helper for the flocks. Rubbing her blossoming belly, she drew Cain's attention to the next child to be born. At least a second child would bring an end to her aching loneliness.

"You'll have a brother or a sister to play with soon enough."

Cain shrugged, the light in his eyes dimming a little. "Play? We'll see."

She eyed his clay forms drying in the sun. "If you hadn't dabbled in the clay pits, we wouldn't have these lovely bowls."

Cain had discovered that if he mixed the clay, he could shape it as he willed. For days, Cain had filled their cave with miniatures of lions, giraffes, foxes, and the mighty hippopotamus which had taken refuge in the river. Adam had grunted when he first saw the creatures, but even he couldn't argue with Cain's skill for sculpting. When her son discovered he could fire the clay and solidify it, Eve found a welcome respite from her basket weaving.

And it was Cain who persuaded Adam to build a simple rock house, one covered in clay. That suggestion had lit Adam's imagination. However, it also meant she saw less and less of her son and her husband. At least it was a worthy sacrifice if both of them got along together as they discussed possible shapes and designs that would best serve the family.

But she had never felt so lonely, finding her only solace with her plants and gardening.

In the days that followed, Cain and Adam appeared to grow closer. Adam had taken his son hunting, determined to try his sleeker spear, tipped with a pointed shard of obsidian. Yet it was Cain's invention, a leather sling attached to the leg bone of a deer used to the launch the spear as straight and as high as a bird, that had earned Adam's complete approval. Such a device ensured Adam could hunt for skins from farther distance, with twice the force.

Cain had basked in his father's praise and had crafted two slings with etched bone covered in delicate designs of deer in flight.

"We'll need fresh tunics and mantles for everyone, especially for the baby coming and the cooler seasons approaching. I could take skins from the sheep or goats, but I'd prefer to save the milk if I can," Adam had told her when she protested the idea of Cain endangering himself during a hunt. Of course, Cain's eyes shone at the prospect of tracking a deer. She hoped the two she loved would eventually find things in common. Her son was so young and vulnerable, and yet so strong-willed.

Evening fell with muted colors as she fed dried chips into the crackling fire. A tiny movement in her belly, so different from the hard kicks Cain used to give, made her smile.

"I feel you, my love. It won't be long now before you arrive." Would she have a boy or a girl? A spark of fear brought back memories of Cain's traumatic birth that had nearly taken her life. Somehow she sensed this child would be easier to deliver.

By the time the sun dipped into the horizon, two shapes emerged into the cave. Cain waved to her as Adam set down his spear. Her husband's features appeared almost pensive as Cain scooted over to sit beside Eve. Her son held his hands over the crackling fire.

"No hunting today?" she asked as she reached for the nearest basket of berries she had gathered earlier, and handed it to Cain.

Adam sank beside her, rummaging through a pouch tied to his waist. He withdrew several nuts, passing them first to her and then Cain. "No. The herd moved south. We followed the tracks as far as we could, but I fear they've moved to a new area of fresh grass."

"Mama, if only you had come with us today! We saw a vast plain beyond our meadow forests. It's ringed with hills in the distance. I want to go back and—"

"We're not exploring, Cain," Adam cut in as he snatched a handful of berries, nearly crushing them in his clenched grip. "I've made that very clear to you. We stay near our home. We've more important things to do here than to wander into the horizon."

Cain jutted out his jaw in defiance. However, he lowered his voice to a mutter. "One day I will return to that plain. You can't stop me. Not when I'm older and as big as you."

Eve felt Adam tense beside her. How could they truly prevent Cain from leaving if he so chose?

"Maybe we could explore as a family during our day of rest. Remember how you took me swimming with the turtles in Eden?" She turned to Adam. "We tasted joy on those days of rest. Why not try it again when the moon wanes?"

Adam grimaced as if the thought were repugnant.

"It's because we have to sacrifice," Cain added, a challenge in his tone, before he tossed the nuts into his mouth. The sound of loud chewing, far louder than she cared for, filled the cave.

Adam gave a derisive snort as he folded his arms across his chest. "I won't exchange what is necessary and important for a moment of idleness. We must sacrifice together as a family."

She sighed, her hopes for the two of them bonding together evaporating like the morning mist that watered the grounds.

"We'll talk no more of it," she conceded, feeling more divided than ever. If only she could have peace in her home. As if to agree, the baby in her womb fluttered gently.

When the moon shone full and bright, a second son was born to Eve. This delivery was far easier, just as she had hoped for, and the boy, whose black hair and narrow eyes reminded her of Adam, lay contented against her breast.

She experienced discomfort with this birth, but it was swiftly overshadowed with the joy of a child yet again in her arms. How she had missed the feel of a tiny body snug next to her own. Hearing her infant's sighs and murmurs proved that all was well with the world. The sweetness of feeling so connected to another person made her feel wanted again. Needed. With a fire crackling, sending a rosy glow over the walls, she felt a rare sense of contentment in her cave.

"He looks so much like you, Adam," she breathed before pressing a kiss against the wee head full of black hair, so unlike Cain's baldness when he was born.

Adam smiled, his eyes crinkling at the corners. He lay his hand against his newborn son's head and fingered the strands of hair. "He'll be a sturdy child. I can sense it. How well you've done, Eve."

She turned to see Cain, who sat with his arms looped around his knees, hugging them close to his narrow chest. His gaze slid from hers.

"Would you like to see your baby brother, Cain?"

He mumbled something unintelligible before rising from the ground to shuffle toward her. He did not touch the baby.

"What shall we name our second son?" she asked as she shifted the infant in her arms to nurse. How contented this little one appeared, his mouth twitching as if to smile at her.

"Abel," Adam answered promptly.

Breath. It was a sobering name choice, fleeting and fragile. Yet necessary to live.

"Abel," she repeated as she watched her baby move to nurse. "You will bring us much happiness."

Without another word, Cain stalked toward his animal skins and flung them over his shoulder. He rolled to face the cave wall, his thin frame hunched into himself.

She opened her mouth to call to her eldest, to reassure him of her love, but Adam's whisper stopped her. "Pay him no heed, Eve. He is jealous. He cannot be the first in everything. It is good for him to share our affection, or he will grow up to be prideful. You have so much love to give. Soon Cain will understand and grow to appreciate his brother."

Was Adam right? She kept silent since the hour was late and exhaustion filled her. But as the snores of Adam soon filled the cave and the baby at her chest fell into a milk-glutted sleep, she couldn't rest, not with the troubling image of Cain's sullen retreat echoing in her thoughts.

CHAPTER FOURTEEN

Three years later

Eve etched the constellations onto the cave wall with a white stone that left a streak of chalky residue. On a whim, she also marked each passing day with a small fleck of white to mark the passage of time.

Outside the cave, the wind felt unusually colder. She tucked the white stone into one of her baskets and pulled out a deerskin so worn and thin that it easily wrapped around her shoulders as a second layer. Adam, who had returned from the river with his hair wet, stopped to study her work lining the wall.

"I want to know how much time passes and track when I need to plant," she explained to Adam when he reached out with a finger to touch her efforts, only to smudge one mark by accident.

He offered her an apologetic look. "That's a good idea. I've been tracking the constellations as well, to put them on the cave wall—it will teach our sons how to study the sky."

Abel reached out and hugged her knees, offering her an impish grin. She smiled in return, amused when her small son retrieved the white stone from the basket and traced images on the lower portion of the wall. How tiny he seemed compared to Cain. But Cain had shot up like the weeds surrounding her garden this past season, tall and prickly, overshadowing everything.

Adam paused at the doorway of the cave, his gaze pinned on Abel's dimpled hands sketching on the jagged surface. Despite the texture of the cave wall, the deer took shape, leaping as one across a small stretch of meadow.

"Amazing how realistic, especially from someone so young," Adam exclaimed as he bent to study the animals. He reached out and tousled Abel's long curls. "Well done. What a gift our son has."

Abel hardly spoke, instead seemingly content to listen and observe everything around him. It was difficult to know what thoughts might reside behind those bright eyes, now a brilliant green, just like his father's. Every day, Abel resembled Adam more and more. Quiet and serious, with precious few words to offer. He continually toddled after his father, wanting to watch the sheep. Adam had swung his son onto his shoulders despite her protests. Despite this boon, Adam still forbade the family from wandering. Abel listened to his father's commands with eyes wide and serious. Rarely did her youngest rebel against anything she or Adam said.

Cain, of course, ducked into the forest more often of late, with a spear strapped to his back. Like her, he abhorred the confines of the cave and the walls, preferring to explore what he could, when he could. Adam at least had Abel's undivided attention, pointing out the differences of the animals and how to examine them for illness.

No one loved animals more than Adam and Abel. Such care was clear in the sketch's detail, the antlers remarkably lifelike despite Abel's age.

"What's wrong with the wall?" Cain asked as he ducked his head to avoid the low cave entrance. He ground to a halt to see why Adam had paused from work.

"Your brother sketched deer in flight," Adam answered readily as he studied the chalk drawing. "It's quite remarkable."

Cain blinked twice. Then he leaned forward to study the sketch, just as Adam had done moments prior. He flexed his lean fingers at his side, moving forward to the wall. With one sweep, he blurred the sketch, smearing white dust against his fingers and palm, stopping only to wipe the chalk against the sides of his tunic.

Eve opened her mouth to protest, but not a single word came to mind. Numbly, she stared at her eldest son, who retreated without a second glance.

"Why would you do such a thing?" She had finally found her tongue.

"I didn't like it. Do I need more of a reason?" He curled his upper lip, the gesture and disdain dripping from his tone somehow reminding her of the serpent in the garden. The hair on her skin rose in response.

"Come with me." Adam placed his hand on Cain's shoulder and steered him out of the cave and into the harsh, bright sunlight.

Cain's voice rose louder, as if he intended to spar. "I don't want to build a house with you today. Why can't I get the morning off to go swimming in the river? Why does Abel get special treatment and I don't?"

"You went swimming yesterday, remember? I let you have the entire afternoon to yourself, just as you asked. You can still swim later this evening if we carry the rock before the sun moves too far to the east." Adam sounded tired, resigned even.

Pain stabbed her chest at the sound of so much pent-up frustration from her eldest. Why was Cain never happy these days? She tried so hard to reach him, to please him. After all, as her first child and her miracle boy, wasn't he the one meant to be the deliverer? The one her Father had promised would come, rescuing her and the children to come from the serpent?

But no true deliverer would act in such a thoughtless way.

Eve felt thin arms wrap around her knees. She reached down and picked up Abel, breathing deeply to control the rush of anger coursing inside of her.

How could her eldest intentionally hurt his own kin? Of course, Adam hadn't really praised Cain's clay sculptures and had instead lavished praise on a young boy. Truthfully, the clumsy animals, though interesting in their own way, didn't showcase the innate skill of Abel.

No, Adam wasn't quite fair, but then again, neither was Cain's response. Why did Adam not see what his eldest son needed most? A father's approval.

Abel nestled against her neck, wrapping his arms around her. She felt his heartbeat slow, matching hers. How easy this child was, so meek and quiet. It was all too easy to get caught up in Cain's constant angst and forget her youngest.

She clasped her youngest. "I'm sorry, Abel. Cain was wrong to ruin your drawings. Your father was right—your deer were beautiful. Would you like to try again?"

Abel leaned back from her embrace, just enough for her to catch a glimmer of tears in his large green eyes. He nodded and she let him slide free to the rock floor.

To her delight, he unfurled his fist, where one of the white stones lay safe. She sat down on the palm fronds and animal skins, watching as his chubby hands drew the deer a second time. It was a gift, offering a glimpse into the way he saw the world—one full of delight and beauty. Just as Adam had a way with animals and thinking of new ways to improve their lives, and she and Cain had their way with gardening, God had blessed Abel with a unique talent. How wonderful to realize her littlest saw beauty everywhere, regardless of how dark the world had become.

She leaned against the wall and lost herself to the moment of enjoying her son's play. A tiny flutter answered in her belly, and a giggle broke free from her. Abel paused, his latest deer sketch showcasing a messy line.

"It's all right, darling boy, I think you will have a new playmate soon enough. What would you like, a sister or a brother?"

"Sister," Abel lisped, to her shock.

A chuckle bubbled up within her at the surprisingly honest answer. But as she rummaged through her baskets for additional fruit and roasted grains to bring to Adam and Cain, her heart clenched yet again. Would a daughter truly bring peace to her home? She fervently hoped so.

With Abel in tow, Eve surveyed the walled garden and the small house taking shape beneath Adam's care.

After digging a series of holes in the ground, Adam had inserted a tall bundle of reeds in each cavity. Once the bundles were all firmly inserted, the ones opposite each other would be bent over and tied at the top to form a roof. For a front barrier, a reed mat would be draped over an opening. The house was round, the walls nearly to her shoulder.

She left Abel to sit on the grass and edged sideways into the narrow opening leading to the main room.

It was far smaller than the cave.

But just as her heart sank, she noticed unusual grooves placed at even intervals along the wall. A hand touched her shoulder, and she spun around to see Adam with a rare grin.

He pointed to the ceiling with a tanned finger. "I made openings for light. Just for you. And we can remove sections of the roof, so you can sleep beneath the stars as we once did. You'll always see something of nature, wherever you turn."

He did this for her? He held her gaze, something bright and lovely shimmering in his eyes. Something that made her shiver all over again, the way she had when they slept on the hill together within Eden.

"I've missed that hill of ours," she admitted. "I've often thought of it."

He captured her hand, his grip strong and his voice husky as he drew her close. "Me too."

Perhaps more might have been said or done judging from the heated way Adam looked at her, but a rustle near the opening of the door revealed Abel watching.

She hid a smile when Adam sighed and stepped back from her.

"What a clever idea to create openings in the roof and walls," she said as she carefully ran her fingers against the rough stone and the damp mud, which, in places, remained fresh.

"It was Cain's inspiration. He deserves much of the praise for thinking of how to bring in more sunlight. We can add a wicker covering to provide a barrier, or animal skins. In the hotter seasons, we can all sleep exposed to the sky. The cave can remain a shelter for Mia and the rest of the flock, or for us when the seasons change. Nothing will be wasted, and you'll still be quite close to your garden and the field."

She found Cain outside the new structure, leaning against a tree and munching on the nuts and berries she had foraged in the early morning.

"You've created something truly remarkable," she told him.

He shrugged before tossing the last of the berries into his mouth. When he finished eating, he straightened his shoulders. "I wanted to design a bigger house, but Father says we've exhausted most of the river rocks close to us. There aren't enough to construct with, especially with the rebuilding of the rock wall. I wondered about using the clay near our home. What if we used mud? We could shape it into anything we wanted."

She patted him on the cheek. "If there is a way to do something, you'll be the one to figure it out first. Both you and your father are so alike, always dreaming of how to tame the land."

It was not entirely her way, this conquering of the meadows, the forest, and everything in between. She still winced whenever Adam used fire to clear out the dead brush.

Cain captured her hand and squeezed it hard. "Thank you, Mama. Thank you for believing in me."

"You are my eldest. My precious son. Why wouldn't I delight in you? I believe God has splendid plans for you. You'll see, soon enough, one day."

She rested a comforting hand on Cain's shoulder and felt him tense with her proclamation. He was nearly as tall as she was, his frame growing so much this past season, with the edge of his stained tunic barely skimming the top of his knees. And though he was young, so very young, how quickly he changed with the passing moons waxing and waning.

He stepped to the side, ducking his head so that his long hair fell over his eyes. She lowered her hand, wanting more than anything to hug and draw him close, but also fearing he would reject her.

If only she could reach him. If only she could convince him that he had great value.

"Cain, I love you."

He looked over his shoulder, his mouth quirked with a half smile. "I love you too, Mama." But as he left her to return to the construction of the house, another memory hovered in her mind. One in which she brushed aside her Father's quiet voice.

CHAPTER FIFTEEN

In the days that followed, the first mud bricks proved to be a complete disaster. Eve knelt on the ground, shaping the mud with her fingers, while Cain did the same. He frowned at the original attempts now littering the ground, chunks which had easily crumbled under pressure. Since their previous conversation, he had tried different variations of mud, rock, and clay mixed together. All to no avail.

He flung the nearest dried brick against the nearest tree, scattering the birds into flight. "It's hopeless!"

She placed her hand on his arm, hoping to soothe the smoldering frustration within him. "Not true. Look how long it took for your father to learn to build the farm you see and for me to weave sturdy baskets and spin sheep's wool. We learn by failing, Cain. Many times so, until at last, an idea pushes through and we finally achieve success."

He squinted at her. "But the house, Mama! We'll never be able to finish it. I know you hate living in that damp cave. I wanted so much to give you something better."

Tears flooded her eyes at Cain's earnest declaration. It was in moments such as these that she believed all would end well for her son, that all he needed was more compassion, more understanding, and then he would grow into a noble man.

He sighed heavily as he fingered the remaining clumps of clay. "Father says we can use your sturdiest baskets to carry rocks from farther down the riverbed."

She didn't care for the idea of her baskets soon worn to shreds with such heavy labor, nor did Cain, from the appearance of it. A grunt escaped him as he tossed aside the ruined brick. One chunk of clay caught her attention. Grass and twigs embedded in it added to the lumpy shape.

She held it up, studying it from every angle before dashing it to the ground. The clay didn't shatter as much as Cain's brick. "What if you mixed grass with the bricks?"

He picked up her piece, his mouth pursed as he tried to pulverize it with his clenched fist. When he raised his head, an affable grin broke across his features, dimpling his cheeks and chasing away the anger. "Trust my mama to solve a problem with her plants."

Eve chuckled. Soft laughter rippled from behind her as she turned just in time to see Abel holding Adam's hand. Together, they approached Eve and her eldest.

"Where were you both?" she asked, while forcing her tone to remain neutral.

Adam ruffled his youngest's hair. "Abel wanted to the see the sheep in the meadow, so I took him."

Cain stiffened at the quiet declaration. Eve wanted nothing more than to protest her husband's careless remark. Why the favoritism? Did Adam not remember how strict he was with Cain in the earlier days?

Adam didn't seem to notice his elder son's response, and instead, lifted Abel high in his arms, pausing long enough to toss him in the air and catch him. Abel squealed with delight, clapping his hands. "Baa, baa," her youngest mimicked the sheep.

Without another word, Cain rose and stalked away from the clay bricks baking beneath the blistering sun.

Adam let Abel slide to the ground. "Did I say something wrong?"

She folded her arms tight across her chest. "You hardly played with Cain during the earliest years of his life, and now you show Abel the very meadow Cain begged to explore. How can you be so thoughtless?"

Adam's eyebrows shot upward. "What are you talking about?"

"You praise Abel's drawings in the cave but ignore Cain's clay animals. You make Cain work every waking moment, except for our day of rest. It's unfair that you put a burden on him while playing with your youngest."

Her husband paused, glancing over his shoulder to see Cain, who by now had disappeared into the forest. Adam turned to her, his voice low and frustrated. "You're not being entirely truthful, Eve. I have given him plenty of space and rest. As for those early years after Eden, have you forgotten that we were starving? I didn't know if we would survive. And if I remember correctly, he ran off more than once. He was so willful, and I didn't want him to end up like you or me."

Yes, Cain had had a disturbing habit of taking whatever he wanted, when he wanted. But she reasoned she had done the same in Eden. Adam's keen assessment brought a flush of shame to her neck and cheeks.

"Regardless, you've not been fair to Cain."

Her husband palmed the back of his neck. "I never meant to hurt him. Never. I want him to grow into an honorable man. But sometimes it feels like there is something inside of him, a darkness, and I've tried so hard to discipline it out of him."

"It's the same darkness inside of us too."

Adam cast her a glance of pure agony. "I know, Eve. Believe me, I've wanted to banish it from my soul. No matter what I do, it's still there. If I can help my children avoid the same mistakes I made, why wouldn't I guide them? I want Cain to know what it was like to walk with God. But there are days when he brushes off my stories as if they were nothing but the serpent's lies. Besides, I cannot give Cain enough recognition or praise to satisfy him. Don't you see that? I praised his efforts earlier with the house, and he ignored me. Now that he is nearly as tall as me, he is fickle and moody, challenging my every decision. One day, our son will lead our family, long after you and I are gone. And if God promised a deliverer through our offspring, then surely our eldest must be raised to such a task."

It was the frankest admission she had heard her husband utter in the years since the banishment. The idea of Cain existing in the world without her or Adam brought a pang of fear. Nor had she realized that Adam had attempted to reach Cain, even if clumsily.

What if Cain wasn't the promised one? What if she had it all wrong? Surely God wouldn't wait too long to send a deliverer, would He? Surely He would rescue them all very, very soon.

She persisted, determined to reclaim some sense of peace. "Don't you think compassion might be a better response for our eldest, especially if he is so temperamental?"

Adam shook his head, his jaw jutting outward. "What you offer isn't compassion. I'll speak no more of it."

In the golden hour of the morning, Eve watched her husband prepare the altar for yet another sacrifice. Their argument several days prior continued to haunt her. Adam saw her as too soft, too emotional. Too ready to overlook an offense and make excuses for her sons. Maybe he even thought her weak, a prospect that stoked a flicker of resentment burning in her chest.

Well, she thought him too hard, too demanding, and far too rigid, with his lists of requirements so difficult to achieve, one might as well quit. Sometimes, he reminded her of the stubborn old rooster who strutted along the rock wall lining the field and garden, stopping only to screech at the rising dawn.

The argument between them was worn and old, like the tunic she had left Eden with, now fragile and thin to the touch, and stretched out from far too much use. Yet she couldn't quite release that garment into the fire. How was it that the man who had once been the perfect partner for her could be so exasperating, so completely wrong on so many issues, and be ridiculously stubborn? Why had God brought her Adam and not someone else?

Father, of course, remained silent on the matter.

And that was another thing that troubled her. She mostly spoke of God as her Father. But Adam no longer did so, as if he had no right to claim such a link. Yet, as she watched Adam bow before the altar with his hands trembling and outstretched, she could see the love and deep longing within him for their Father.

Once again, Adam beseeched God to take the sacrifice as an atonement for their sins. She closed her eyes, overwhelmed, when memories flashed through her mind. The angel with his sharp sword. The serpent's mocking laughter. And Father's grief when He asked them why they had hidden.

Could Adam's sacrifice truly bring them closer to their Father? As always, she reached out with her mind, pleading for God to respond.

If only I could hear Your voice again. I miss You so much that it aches.

A tear dripped down her cheek, and she dashed it away. As she raised her head, she saw Abel's expression of awe as he stared at the blood-stained altar where a lifeless lamb bore her shame.

Abel glanced at her and reached out his hand to clasp hers.

"Why do you cry, Mama?" he whispered.

She shook her head, too overwhelmed to speak by the sight of an innocent creature slain on her behalf. Every time Adam sacrificed, her heart felt as though it would rend. How could she possibly bridge the gap between her and her Father after what she had done? How could she repair what she had so easily ruined?

Her throat closed tightly when Cain didn't bother to hide his snort. He shuffled backward, as if ready to flee the altar. When she frowned at him, he rolled his eyes with a slight huff of exasperation.

"It's cruel to kill that poor lamb," her eldest muttered through clenched teeth. "Cruel and pointless."

She had thought the same as Cain when Adam had first sacrificed. But now? Was this truly the way? She couldn't help but wonder…

Her husband missed the exchange as he bowed his head in reverence, no doubt lost in thoughts or memories of Eden.

She returned her attention to her eldest, who was now scratching his ear, as if completely unimpressed with the sacrifice. She ought to say something to Cain. Perhaps she ought to correct him, but the argument with Adam remained far too fresh. What to do?

So instead, she held her tongue and kept her thoughts to herself.

CHAPTER SIXTEEN

The third pregnancy brought plenty of surprises and laughter. For once, Eve felt as though her Father had heard her quiet pleas and blessed her womb with a double portion. And though this delivery brought suffering, with not one but two girls, she nearly wept for joy. Two exquisite girls. Calah and Edina.

In the secret hours of the previous night, when the cave was filled with the sounds of snoring, she had fretted on her mat, wondering if her sons would have more brothers to contend with. But with this delivery, Cain had joined in the festivities. He even held one of his sisters in his long arms.

"Calah," he whispered to the sleeping newborn. "Sweet, tiny Calah."

The daughter at Eve's breast, Edina, fussed, her rosy mouth puckering with frustration when she failed to latch, and a wail filled the cave. Eve shifted her infant and smiled at her growing family, who crowded close to the see the miracle of new life. Abel hung back, but his wide grin with a missing tooth brought a smile to Eve. How happy her middle child appeared. Instead of sulking, Abel carefully crept forward to watch his sisters.

"Mama, they are so pretty. Are you thirsty? Do you want anything? Can I help you?"

His eager questions warmed her heart.

"No, Abel. You help your father with the chores. That will be more than enough."

He pressed a kiss against her head before finding a spot on the animal skins to give her more space in the crowded cave.

She hoped they would move soon to the new house once Adam and Cain constructed the roof, but for now, Eve planned to rest in her familiar space, draped with woven mats and leather skins. Adam at least allowed Cain more hours to himself, pushing less and less for so much to be done. The house took longer to build, but the arguing was also less and less.

Perhaps her husband had listened to her after all. His challenge to her continued to bring a flush of guilt.

Pushing aside the uncomfortable thought, she glanced down at the baby nursing at her breast. Edina, with her head full of dark hair, seemed to be the hungrier twin, drinking and drinking her fill of milk.

Adam reached for Calah, who opened her mouth to cry, but Cain pivoted on his heel, while holding his sister close.

"She needs to eat, Cain," Adam warned as he held out his arms.

Pushing out his full bottom lip, Cain reluctantly relinquished his hold of the baby.

Placing Calah with Eve, Adam stepped backward, his frown deepening.

"Is there milk enough for both of them?"

Eve chuckled despite her exhaustion. "If need be, I'll make more."

But as Edina struggled to nurse, a moment of fear struck Eve. What if her daughters carried a rivalry? What if, as a mother, she couldn't give enough of herself to each child?

At last, Eve had enough sense of the seasons, waning and waxing moons, and constellations spinning in the sky, that she roughly charted out a reasonable approximation of the passage of the days. Every night, she looked up at the stars and thought of her Father, so silent and so far away. Once, she had reached up her hand to touch the sky before snatching it to her chest, feeling all the more foolish.

He saw her—she knew that much. But had He tired of her? His silence stretched on and on as the days passed, yet His promise to send a deliverer kept the flicker of hope warm inside of her.

When Calah and Edina reached the age of three years, the two could hardly look more different, or act more unlike each other. Whatever secrets and wisdom Eve had gleaned from her sons now hardly applied with her daughters.

She knew how to bathe a slippery newborn in the river. She knew not to be alarmed, unlike the first time, when Cain had fussed and drooled, until at last two teeth pushed out of his gums. She knew how to treat stomach rashes and how to mash food to feed a growing baby.

But to tend to a daughter's emotions…

This was new territory, full of new frustrations.

Edina, like Cain, grew into a strong-willed and domineering child, organizing the household in ways that best suited her.

"Bossy," Adam described his daughter, though not without affection. Calah, however, moved like the gentle breeze. Her temperament suited Abel's winsome manner, but unlike Adam and Abel, Calah loved to listen and chat with Eve throughout the day.

At long last, Eve had found a child that fit into the secret longings of her heart. No favorites, of course. She could not choose among her children, but Calah was the one who was content to sit with her and listen while weaving reeds with her nimble fingers to form baskets.

Calah would often plead, "Tell me another story about the garden and your Father, Mama. Tell me about the mighty trees and the serpent."

This morning was no exception as she rolled her spindle between her palm and thigh, stretching and compressing the wool into longer threads. A fair amount of spun wool gathered on top of the whorl as she ran it back and forth. Adam had carved a bone dowel for her, allowing her to insert it through the spinning whorl with the fluffy wool attached to it. Over the seasons, she had experimented with the raw fibers of plants but now preferred the wool for its comfort and ease of use. Her daughters watched her spindle, their mouths rounding with wonder as the speed of the wool snaked round and round at the top of the whorl.

The story still made Eve's throat tighten, but she made herself recount the first moments, days, and later weeks leading up to the serpent's betrayal.

"Is that wicked old thing still out there in the forest?" Calah asked as she sat cross-legged on the mat.

"No," a deepening voice answered before Eve could. Edina and Calah whirled to see Cain enter the house. He made a face and stuck out his tongue when he spied the three of them huddled together. "But if you wander too far into the forest, you'll never know what you might find." Snapping his teeth, he lunged for them, swinging out his arms to snatch either twin.

The girls squealed with mock terror while Cain winked at them. He stopped short of Calah and tugged her long locks. Her hair had lightened to warmer hues than Eve's black curls. Dark brown with hints of auburn when the sun hit the strands just right.

His expression softened, but it was Edina leaped off the skins and tugged on his arm, drawing him away from Calah.

"Tell us another scary story, Cain!"

He waggled his eyebrows, clearly enjoying being the center of the twins' attention. "There is a mighty lion who likes to eat children and foxes, crunching them bone by bone, and then there is a crocodile who suns on the bank of the river, big enough to swallow you whole—"

"That's enough for one day," Eve interrupted as she rose from her reed mat. "Keep up with those stories, and Calah and Edina will never leave the house."

He smirked in return as he snatched a leather satchel hanging from a peg on the wall.

"What are your plans today?" she asked after a moment's hesitation.

He slung the satchel over his shoulder. "I'll plant the fields. Abel will help Father with the animals. After that, who knows?"

She nodded, troubled again by the distance Cain maintained from Abel. "Will you keep an eye out for your brother and make sure he doesn't get into trouble?"

Cain didn't answer her question as he strode from the shadowed room into the bright outdoors. She left her doorway open, the thick screen made from branches and reeds secured at night. Not once did he slow his steps.

"Cain?" she called out, but he was gone.

Eve packed a satchel loaded with apples, nuts, and speckled eggs. Calah walked beside her while Edina ran ahead, chasing the yellow butterflies that hovered in the breeze.

Cain had planted seeds in groupings. Peas and beans with tall grains or vibrant sunflowers in individual groupings, with leafy greens and cabbages in between. She had discovered that certain plants repelled insects while inviting bees to pollinate. Some plants invigorated the soil, while the others provided shade for weaker plants.

She watched as Cain dug into the ground with his bone tools. Several paces away, Adam and Abel fussed over a ewe giving birth.

"May I help Abel?" Calah tugged on Eve's tunic. "I want to see the babies!"

"Just for a quick moment, and then come back. I still need you to weed."

Calah beamed before joining Abel and Adam, leaving Edina with Eve.

"I'd rather help Cain," Edina said as she wrinkled her pert nose. "I've seen plenty of stinky lambs born already."

Eve couldn't help but chuckle. By help, Edina would likely direct Cain, much to his annoyance. Already, her daughters showed their preferences, Edina drifting toward Cain and Calah toward Abel.

She touched her daughter on the shoulder. "I also suspect there'll be plenty of peas for you to enjoy in the meantime."

Her medicinal garden and Adam's field had saved their lives. The hens laid their eggs in the safety of a separate pen, and the fruit trees nearby provided a variety of sweetness. Her stomach no longer growled with hunger as it had during the first years. Nor did she have to count out the painfully meager portions, keeping the mushiest samples for herself so that her family might eat.

But when she approached the wall, her gaze collided with Cain's. He scowled at her, his hands on his hips.

"What's wrong?" she asked, dreading his answer.

He pointed to the nearest cluster of plants. And then another. "Blight. It's taken about half the crop."

She bent over to study the stalk of the sunflower he pointed to, noting the black speckles covering the green. "I've never seen this before. Can we cut what is rotten and save the rest of the plants?"

Cain emitted a low moan as he shielded his eyes from the sun while surveying the rest of the field. "I suppose we will have no choice. We won't have enough food to harvest otherwise."

"Edina and I will start at the southern section and work our way to you."

"Where's Calah?" Cain interjected, sounding peeved.

She hesitated when he turned from the crops to search for his other sister. His favorite, as it was becoming clearer by the day. Something akin to dread welled up within her as she followed his line of sight.

"She's with Abel, watching the ewe give birth."

Cain grunted his displeasure. "We'll need everyone in the fields if we are to save the crops."

She didn't answer, and Edina, who eagerly followed Cain's every step, kept her brother distracted with constant chatter.

"Don't you think you ought to remove more of the black leaves?" Edina pointed to one particular leaf.

"Not sure it will make much difference in the end, but by all means, pull the leaf yourself," Cain retorted sharply.

Edina's bottom lip trembled, but she propped her fists on her hips, mimicking her brother's fierce stance. "You first."

Eve concentrated on the plants in front of her, fingering one green leaf between her fingers. She sensed the blight was dangerous, eating the plants from within and spreading from one plant to the next until soon the entire field would be contaminated.

It wasn't enough to pluck the leaves and cast them on the ground. She needed to remove the tainted produce. Burn it, perhaps.

Another memory brought a tremble to her fingers. When fleeing Eden, a decay had spread across the landscape, wilting and changing what was once good into something stained with death.

Wasn't this how sin spread? In her. In Adam. It ruined whatever it touched. It crept into every corner and lurked, like a poisonous mold.

The sound of arguing filled the garden. She raised her head to see Edina and Cain clashing over which row to work on next. Edina tossed her brown curls and stomped her foot. Not at all intimidated by her brother's size or age, she continued to direct him.

"Don't throw the leaves on the ground, Edina. Throw them in the basket," Cain growled at his sister.

Edina sniffed loudly as she tossed a leaf into the basket on the ground. "You don't have to sound so mean."

And now, sin in her children. A shuddering sigh escaped Eve. All she wanted was a taste of peace to enjoy during the quiet morning. Was that too much to ask?

She raised her voice loud enough to ring across the field. "Stop it, both of you. I'll be the only one tending crop myself if you stand there fighting with each other."

"Edina never listens," Cain muttered under his breath. "Unlike Calah."

Edina's large hazel eyes filled with tears as she tugged at the ruined leaves. "I do listen," she protested. "I'm the one who is here in this awful garden. Not Calah."

"Enough," Eve stated firmly. Was she to endure yet another fight this morning?

"It's hopeless," Cain ground out through his clenched teeth as he shot a withering glance in Eve's direction. "Your pruning will amount to nothing."

"Maybe," Eve answered. "I often ask Father for help when I tend to the plants. Why don't we ask Him?"

Cain arched his eyebrow, the curl of his lip so contemptuous, she was almost sorry she suggested it. "I've yet to hear Him speak, Mama."

Regardless of her son's disdain, she reached out with her mind and asked God for help. How could she make her son see that the Creator loved him?

As the sun mellowed, dipping into the horizon, she had gathered several baskets of ruined plants. After dumping the contents on the ground far beyond the walled field, she waited for Cain to return with his fire rocks and dried bark to kindle a flame.

He knelt on the ground, striking the rocks with a vehemence. A flash of light and the strips of bark smoldered. With a bit more coaxing, a fire soon ate at the dried sticks, while the green leaves only shriveled and smoked. But eventually the fire won, turning the plants to feathery ashes.

"Why must everything be so hard?" His fingers clenched around the rocks, white with strain. "Why did God allow this blight to happen? I know you and Father want to please Him. Why does He reward your sacrifices this way?"

She reached out and caressed her son's face. "Cain, you know the story better than anyone else. I took the fruit from the Tree of Knowledge of Good and Evil. It was me. And it was your father. And this is the price we pay for our sin."

"It doesn't seem fair. Why did God have to give you a choice? Why did He insist on tempting you with such a test? If He was so loving and good, wouldn't He have provided a way out, an escape? Why must we prove ourselves to Him?"

She had long wrestled with those questions. What a simple solution, to have no choice at all. No free will. No responsibility. If only she could return to Eden and live as she once had. If only she had chosen wisely and ignored the serpent's lies. Lies, she suspected, her son might be listening to as well.

"If there is no choice, it's hardly love, is it? I choose to love you and always will. Yet I can't make you love me. Only you can decide if you will offer love in return."

Her throat tightened as she thought of Abel and Edina. She certainly couldn't make Cain care for his siblings, or Adam, even though she desired that her family would grow closer together, not farther apart.

She continued even though Cain's gaze slid from hers. "Besides, it's about taking responsibility for our choices. I was free to make my choice. Father warned disobedience would result in death, and yet I didn't believe Him."

Cain rested his arms on his knees, his face hard like stone. Edina crept up to Eve and slid her arm through Eve's. Eve kissed her daughter's head. "I'm so sorry, my sweet, sweet children, that sin entered this world because of my choices. I take hope because my Father, your Father as well, promised a way out. He told me He would send a deliverer through my seed. One day, one of mine will rise and strike at death and the serpent."

"When?" Cain raised his eyebrows. "When will this so-called deliverer come and rescue us?"

"I don't know. Some days, I had hoped that he would be you, Cain."

He closed his eyes at her halting admission. "I'm so tired of fighting, Mama. This land, this life, and all that is in it. Don't place this burden on me too. I cannot take it."

His curt answer burned away any lingering hope that he would be the one. Sucking back a sob, she struggled to regain her composure. "You are wrestling with God. How I wish you could have known Father the way I once did. He was so loving and so kind—"

Cain's eyes flared open, hard and bright. "Once," he interjected with so much venom, she reared back. "Perhaps He was that way *once*, but He is certainly no more. No, it's nothing more than a pretty story to entertain Calah and Edina. I, too, once listened to your tales. You told them so convincingly. There were moments when I felt as if I had experienced Eden. Yet how do I know you are telling the truth?"

Shock flooded her at his accusation. "I-I'm not lying. I would never lie to you."

"You don't think I remember how you and Father fought when I was Edina's age? Neither of you were very truthful with each other. I remember only too well. Keep your fireside tales for your daughters. At least they like to be entertained."

She could hardly see him through the sudden wash of tears as he jumped up and fled into the thick shadows of the surrounding forest.

Edina whimpered as she snuggled closer to Eve. "Will he come back, Mama?"

Eve wrapped her arm around her daughter and pulled her close. "Hush, my sweet lamb, Cain always returns. He's just angry right now. He'll be fine after a day or two alone."

But his accusation of her lies…oh, the irony. Hadn't she done something similar to her Father? She had chosen not to believe Him and listened to the serpent instead. Why, oh why, was Cain so much like her? Her beloved child, choosing yet again to be alone, when all she wanted was to draw him close into her arms.

CHAPTER SEVENTEEN

Eve trudged from the field, her limbs aching and her heart even more so. Edina kept silent, her determined gait now faltering, just like Eve's.

No sign of Cain. The sun fled, and night fell, and the forest around Eve came alive with frightening sounds. Once inside the safety of her house, she sat down on the mat with Adam, Abel, and her daughters, explaining what had happened with her eldest.

"Do we look for him?" Abel asked, his green eyes wide with alarm. "I'll go right now."

"We might track him, but it's black outside," Adam answered with resignation as he dipped his hand into a basket of fruit and pulled out a handful of blueberries. "It's too dangerous in the dark. We'll wait for the first light."

Abel nudged the basket of berries closer to his sisters, as if his appetite had fled. "Knowing Cain, he wants to be by himself, but it isn't right."

Adam's gaze collided with Eve's for an instant, worry etched in the fine lines surrounding his eyes. His weary gaze slid away, focusing on the berries in his blue-stained palm.

When had he aged? It wasn't much, really, but the lines were there, deepening into grooves on his forehead. Crinkles at the corners of his green eyes. His strong shoulders slumped as he picked at his food.

She longed to smooth away his expression of worry, but the years passing had widened the divide between them, even if they lived and worked side by side.

After her children went to bed, she sat on the mat near the door and waited as the moon rose high and bright, drifting slowly between the openings near the roof where she saw a glimpse of a star-spangled sky. Hours fled, tracked by the movement of the moon from one side of the house to the other.

And still no sign of Cain.

She wrapped her arms about her knees, determined to wait for her son no matter how long it took. But when her head knocked against her knees, she realized she had fallen asleep.

A hand reached down to touch her shoulder.

"Come to bed," Adam's gruff voice ordered.

"I can't sleep," she whispered back.

"You must. You will wait all night for him, otherwise. And it won't do either of you any good."

She didn't answer his challenge, instead hugging her knees closer to her chest.

"Eve—"

"He accused me of lying about God, Adam. *Me.* His mother. He doesn't really believe either of us. Says he remembers our arguments when he was just a little boy, which fills me with all the more shame. And he thinks your sacrifices are pointless and cruel."

A long silence fell, and the divide seemed to widen between them.

"My sacrifices?" Adam's voice sounded small. "Do you not believe in them?"

"I do believe," she faltered, but her answer was slow enough that she heard her husband's sharp intake of breath. "But our son does not. I don't want him to come to harm out there in the wild. I fear that He is angry at you and God." Her as well, if she was completely honest.

"And you blame me for our son," he said it flatly. "You think I don't care about either of you."

She blamed herself so much it hurt most days. But yes, she blamed Adam. The answer lodged in her throat as the sounds of the night filled in the gap.

An audible swallow came from him.

"Go to bed, Eve." His tone was rough and low.

She wanted to refuse his order. Indeed, a retort burned on the tip of her tongue. As she rose from the entrance of the door and stumbled toward the mat, he didn't follow her. Instead, she heard rustling from the other side of the circular main room.

Dimly, she saw him thrust aside the leather curtains and head out into the night with a spear in hand.

Sunlight filtered through the opening in the roof. Eve rolled over on the mat, but instead of her fingers brushing against her husband, she touched only air. Several days and nights had passed in which she slept alone without her husband's long form next to her.

Quickly, she sat up. Calah and Edina lay together, snuggled close as if to keep each other warm. Abel lay with his arm pillowed behind his head, his breathing deep and even. How like Adam in a picture of younger, carefree days. But instead of smiling at the cozy scene, she felt a renewed sense of urgency flood through her.

She tiptoed out of the house so as not to awaken her sleeping children and headed outside into the pale dawn. As she surveyed the grounds, now covered with a thick, rolling mist, as heavy as the clouds above, her pulse raced when she realized neither her eldest nor her husband had returned home.

Where were they? Had Cain or Adam experienced danger?

Fear brought a tremble to her fingers as she considered her words a few nights ago. Could God heal the fractures in her family?

How hurt Adam sounded at her accusations. But not once had he acknowledged his role in the garden of Eden, or in their home. A sliver of blame for what had happened at the tree remained between them, festering and poisoning. How could she forget how quickly Adam blamed her for the stolen fruit?

Perhaps Cain had reason to doubt her story. Perhaps she had made too many mistakes for God to seek her.

She approached the field where she and Edina had worked, and in the damp air, her children's previous bickering faintly echoed, stealing any peace.

Father, please help. Bring Adam and Cain home safely.

The resulting hush that lay over the field and meadow brought more tears to her eyes. She would never get used to this separation, this silence from God. Dashing away at the wetness on her cheeks, she fingered the nearest plants she had helped Cain prune. To her surprise, fresh growth peeked through where the ruined leaves had been torn free—a healing that was beyond the normal.

She weaved in between the rows, inspecting plant after plant, her vexation giving way to astonishment.

"Thank You, thank You, Father," she said out loud.

"Mama?" Abel reached her side, staring at the plants with her. He nearly reached her shoulder. Scratching his head, he stared at the crop. A sleepy Edina yawned from behind him, and Calah slipped her arm into Eve's, standing on tiptoes to see better.

Eve plucked a leaf and showed her children. "Look. Our Father restored the plants. Cain didn't believe me, but God removed the blight when I asked."

Abel laughed, the sound shocking after days of tense waiting. But unlike Cain's derision, Abel's laughter was purely rejoicing. He took the leaf from her and held it up to the light before passing it to his sisters. "I see it. He is a good Father, Mama. I believe your stories of Eden. I will always believe it, and one day, I'll tell my children."

She stiffened for the briefest moment. Of course, Abel heard her and Adam's argument in the dark. Privacy wasn't exactly the best in their tight quarters.

But before she could answer, her younger son wrapped his arm about her and pulled her close, soundly kissing her cheek.

He motioned for his sisters to follow him. "Come on, sleepyheads, let's do some weeding."

Calah didn't need to be asked twice as she ran back to the house to find a basket to help her brother. But Eve couldn't help but notice how, like her, Edina searched the forest where the dense fog retreated as the sun warmed the land.

She patted Edina's frail shoulder. "If God can heal our crops, then let's trust Him with Cain and your father."

Edina nodded, but her mouth pinched further.

Eve joined with her children, her fingers digging into the damp soil. Dirt stained the tips of her fingers, and the scent of spicy earth hit her nostrils. One of her favorite scents. The morning proved to be a pleasant one in the absence of her eldest. She banished that traitorous thought as soon as it crossed her mind, but the niggling thought persisted.

Cain brought conflict, as if he didn't know of any other way to connect with his family.

Edina ducked when Abel tossed a weed over his shoulder. It struck Calah on the shoulder. Her bright laughter filled the garden. Abel glanced to see his sister brush the dirt from her tunic. She picked up her plucked weed and threw it at him, landing smack in the center of his chest.

"Oh no, you don't." He stood to his full height, his mischievous grin dimpling either side of his cheek. The girls squealed when he pretended to give chase.

Eve laughed with her children, and oh, the sound of joyful children—how good it was!

She wiped her eyes, this time from laughter instead of tears, and pivoted on her heel to gather more weeds.

Adam stood at the edge of the wall enclosing the crop.

Her laughter died when she spied him. His eyes, brilliant as ever, studied her. She froze, bracing herself for battle. Did he resent her previous words? Her accusations?

He rested his spear against the wall and vaulted over the rock barrier, his form just as strong and youthful as she remembered. Questions bubbled up as she glanced about for Cain, her movements almost frantic.

"He's safe, Eve," Adam said when he reached her. A hint of a smile warmed the severe lines of his face, but it did nothing to reassure her.

"Where is he?"

"Alone. But safe, I promise. He has much to ponder. Believe me, the quiet and rest will be good for him."

She shook her head as she placed her basket on the ground. "No. I've got to see him and talk with him. I need—"

Adam captured her cheek with his hand, his palm calloused but warm against her skin. He leaned into her. "Trust me, Eve. Please. He is nearly a man, and one day, he'll have a home of his own. He will not always be with us. You cannot always mother him."

Such a thought was inconceivable. Of course her children would remain close to her, living side by side with one another. But Adam's gaze, full of tenderness, distracted her. She wanted to protest that Adam was wrong and that what her son needed most was the love of a mother, but Adam reached out for her hand and squeezed her fingers gently.

"I want to hear you laugh again, Eve. You are so beautiful when you smile."

Her breath caught at the simple admission, and she saw a glimpse of her husband the way he had once been, when love was new and bright, and the world was full of hope and possibility.

If God could heal the land, surely He could heal her relationships. Surely hope remained.

In the morning that followed Adam's return, a gift awaited her, nestled in a frond, set carefully beside her mat so that it would be the first thing she saw when she opened her eyes. The seed of an avocado, a smooth sphere threatening to roll away, gleamed beneath the rays of the morning sun.

She gasped with delight when she reached for it. In time, the seed would grow to be a tree, and with it, new fruit.

She pressed it against her lips and inhaled the nutty scent, unable to hide her growing smile.

Work resumed, the cycle, the sameness and boredom of it no longer as much a burden. Not when she saw Adam explain to Abel how to smooth one of her salve concoctions onto the leg of an injured lamb who limped. Casting her a wink, Adam scooped a glob of oil from a clay pot and demonstrated how to spread the concoction.

The lamb bleated as Abel reached for it, but it silenced when he smeared the paste onto the leg with careful fingers. Her son's face flushed as he listened intently to Adam's quiet instructions, beaming at last when Adam praised him.

She loved watching them work together.

Oblivious to the rest of the world, they knelt, their heads bent together as they inspected the flock for disease or wounds. Both taking care of the animals, silent and strong as they completed their tasks. Abel's simple joy brought Eve a moment of conviction. He did not know what she or Adam missed after living in a perfect garden. Instead, her second son approached each new day as if it were a gift to be savored. To be cherished.

Did she do the same? Did she savor what she had? As soon as the thought crossed her mind, Adam straightened and looked right at her. A shiver, much like the ones of old, rippled through her.

The next morning, an orchid loaded with purple and white blossoms, its dangling roots exposed, lay on a new frond. She picked up the flower as carefully as she could so as not to disturb the fragile petals. How long had it taken him to free the flower from the soil, and to do so with such care that she could transplant it?

Adam was reminding her of Eden and everything beautiful that had happened there on their hill, their first home. A blush heated her skin as she found a slender tree trunk to wrap the surrounding roots where the orchid would be displayed high for all to see, especially Adam.

Her husband was wooing her.

On the thirteenth day, a figure appeared through the swirling fog coating the field and meadows. Cain had finally returned home. He murmured a greeting to Eve when he entered the field. She had to restrain herself from running to him and smothering him with an embrace.

"We all missed you," she said as she brushed aside a wild curl from his cheek, unable to resist with that gesture at least.

He nodded, a far more subdued version than the Cain she last saw. "I missed you too."

"And your time away—it was good?"

The slightest shudder rippled across his shoulders, so faint she might have imagined it. Now that he was in front of her, she had every opportunity to study him beneath the sunlight. Bluish shadows draped beneath his eyes and his cheekbones slashed, as if he had lost weight. Or perhaps he hadn't, and his appearance was more because of the haunted air he wore.

"It was good, Mama." With that, he left her with more questions than answers and a heart aching in a manner that only a mother could understand.

CHAPTER EIGHTEEN

Many moons passed, bringing the changes of the seasons. The sky above remained blue and endless. The river drew its current, carving out the riverbed into novel forms. Meanwhile, Eve watched her sons grow, their legs lengthening and Cain's shoulders broadening until the leather and woolen tunics she stitched nearly stretched at the seams.

Her eldest changed into a handsome and powerful man at thirty years of age. Different from Adam, yet there were glimpses of her husband to be found in him. Like Adam, Cain continued to dream of conquering the land. He left the house more and more, sometimes even camping beneath the stars alone with nothing more than a spear and his kindling rocks. With bark peeled from trees and dried until powdery and crisp, he tucked the kindling pieces into a small pouch strung about his neck.

Abel grew as well, now twenty years old. Not as tall but just as broad shouldered and always with an amiable smile dimpling his cheeks. If Cain was fire, then Abel was water, soothing and nurturing, settling quarrels between his sisters, fitting so easily into the cracks of her family. Her younger son was a man of few words, but when he did share, the entire family listened. Except for Cain, perhaps.

And if her sons were handsome, then her daughters were even more beautiful. Calah's hair lightened beneath the sun as she alternated between the garden and the multiplying herds of sheep, goats, and hens. Her skin, a dusky hue, deepened beneath the sun. Her eyes, a warm hazel, searched for Abel more and more as of late.

Edina preferred to remain indoors and avoid the heat of the midday, so she remained a paler color. With locks black as night, Edina was just as pretty as her sister, but her mouth, more often than not, remained pulled into a pout.

She took over the sewing, her nimble fingers threading the bone needle with ease. As long as Adam and Abel brought new skins, Edina sewed and wove with a newly designed loom until she stocked the house with a fresh assortment of tunics and mattresses stuffed with moss and long grass. The interior of the circular house felt cramped as Eve's children aged.

Someone was always bumping into another. One morning in particular, Eve tried not to notice when Calah tripped within the cramped confines, the contents of her basket flying. Swiftly, Abel reached out his arm and caught her, setting her back on her feet.

Eve held her breath while the two of them searched each other's gaze. Abel's arm remained pinned around Calah's waist. The air inside the house grew heavy.

Eve's hands hovered over the new basket taking form as she studied her son and daughter. Even Edina paused over the careful stitches of a tunic she mended. Eve glanced at Edina, who merely raised her eyebrows.

Edina had never shared a special bond with Abel. If anything, she spent more time sparring with Cain and testing his will. Yet Eve knew Edina coveted Cain's attention. If only he cared to give it.

Was this blossoming romance part of her Father's plan? God had created her for Adam. There had been no one else to choose. Now, her children had little choice.

Calah's smile hinted that she might have decided. Especially when she made no move to untangle herself from Abel. Instead, she continued to gaze at him until at last, he cleared his throat and released her before hurrying out of the house, leaving the women behind.

Calah lowered her gaze and sank down beside Eve while reaching for another basket to weave.

"I fear we've outgrown our home," Eve remarked quietly as she picked up another reed to insert into the pattern unfolding into a colorful design. The basket, dyed with berry stains, had taken a pleasing shape entwined with dull crimson and deep purple strips of grass.

"I hate this place," Edina blurted. She jabbed the needle attached to the rawhide string into the leather and pulled it through, leaving a neat stitch behind despite the anger leaking from her voice.

"Why?" Calah asked.

Edina scowled, transforming her lovely face into something altogether furious. "It's the same day after day. I'm sick of it. Cain thinks we should move farther downstream. He said there is better land where the river heads east toward a flat area covered with the tallest grass you ever saw. He says it's perfect for fields and animals grazing."

"I think your father wants to stay put," Eve answered. "He will decide whether we will move or not."

Edina snorted as she wrestled with the needle and the leather tunic.

"Your desire will be for your husband." Again, God's warning circled within Eve. No, Adam decided where they lived. He had no desire to transfer everything they owned to a new site. Now that Eve had spent so many years in this land, she no longer had quite the overwhelming urge to explore the craggy hills and follow the path of the mighty river. Regardless, she didn't feel quite at home here either.

"We would have to start over," Calah remarked. "Construct new walls around new fields, and then there would be the homes needing to be built. I don't think any of us has the energy to spare for such a massive undertaking."

It was impossible not to note how Calah said "homes." Already Eve's daughters were dreaming of the future and all the promise it held. Did Calah plan to have a home of her own soon?

But if Eve held back from asking, Edina forged ahead as she pierced the leather again with her needle, nearly jabbing her finger in the process. "Have you and Abel made plans for a home of your own?"

Calah ducked her head, not meeting anyone's gaze. "No, we have not spoken of it. I had always planned to stay close to family. Abel has so much to do. I doubt he thinks of such things either."

Eve patted Calah's arm. "Nothing would please me more than to have my children close to me."

Calah smiled weakly as she picked up a thin reed to insert into her basket.

"Didn't you once say God wanted us to fill the earth?" Edina's sharp question brought a quiver to Eve's chest. "So, why shouldn't we spread out in whatever direction we choose?"

Eve placed her hand on her belly, and the new life within it fluttered in response. "Yes, He commanded us to fill the earth."

Edina's eyes widened when she caught Eve's subtle gesture. "You are going to have another child."

"Hopefully," Eve answered, hating the tremor in her voice. "We shall see soon enough."

In the seasons that had passed, Eve had lost three babies, each miscarrying near the rise of the full moon. And there were many seasons when she felt as though her womb had been closed.

God had promised childbearing would be hard, but losing an infant had proven to be the most painful burden of all. She couldn't imagine such loss extending to the children she had raised and loved. But death hovered near, no matter how hard Adam tried to tame the land or Edina worked to make the house comfortable or Eve searched for the right cures to keep her family safe and strong.

"Are you hurting? Do you want me to harvest the yellow flower?" Calah asked as she twisted the reeds and threaded them into her unfinished basket.

The yellow henbane flowers with thick petals, rising from hairy stems and leaves, could be ingested, or its dried seeds could be sprinkled over a fire, creating a soothing smoke if inhaled into the mouth for toothaches or muscle aches. But not all the plants used for healing could be used indiscriminately. Some, in high quantities, brought terrifying dreams and visions as Eve had learned by mistake. No one touched the herbs until she did—a rule Adam hated. Despite her husband's protests, her Father had given her keen instincts on which plants were safe and which ones were not.

"I'll be fine, Calah. I would prefer to leave the herbs alone. Rest will do me better."

In the past, she pushed herself to the limit, regardless of Adam's muttered protests. But now? She wasn't as energetic as she once was.

"We're rather low on mandrakes," Calah mused as she shoved the unfinished basket next to Eve's collection. "I ought to collect more before the day ends."

Edina's mouth twitched as Calah left the house, but her next words sent a frisson of caution rippling through Eve. "I'm sure my sister will hunt for more than just roots."

CHAPTER NINETEEN

Over the next several seasons, Eve snuck glances at Abel and Calah to discern if any lasting change had occurred. But life mostly continued as it always had, and she heaved a sigh of relief.

Unfortunately, some things in her home never seemed to change. Her husband hardly rested, as was his habit. Adam usually rose first, before dawn, always preoccupied with a new project or two. The enclosed wall and house had lit his imagination on fire. Praising her efforts at collecting seeds, he had taken her storehouse supplies to plant in the soil, extending the fields and planning new enclosures to guard the crops.

The avocado tree unfurled its branches, bringing new fruit. And a peach tree, along with cherries and plums, budded first with flowers and then with exquisite temptations—calling men, birds, and worms alike.

If she plucked the peaches first, just before the flesh got too tender, she avoided the bugs.

"You've recreated a touch of Eden," Adam had told her with a hint of awe the day prior when they had stood beneath the dappled shadows. He had reached out to graze the nearest avocado dangling from the tree branch.

His rare compliment brought another smile to her lips. Her garden and orchard were truly wonderful to behold, but nothing could compare to the home of her heart, now guarded by cherubim. As the years passed, she longed more and more for the peace and simplicity of her former life.

Especially now, when she heard tinkling laughter floating over the field. Adam turned with her, to see Abel bring Calah a newborn lamb to pet. Abel grinned as he leaned into Calah, whispering things only for her to hear. Calah giggled again as she stroked the lamb's head. Then she reached out and tucked a long lock of hair behind Abel's ear. His eyes widened in response and his mouth parted, as if he was speechless.

A tight knot formed in Eve's stomach. Had she looked at Adam the way Calah gazed at Abel, with such adoration? How long ago it all seemed.

Adam grunted beside her, the sound not entirely displeased. "Good. It's about time our children moved on with their lives as they should. Those two will be a fine match for each other."

She wanted to agree, but a sense of unease pervaded when Cain strode past Calah and Abel, deliberately steering their way and interrupting the conversation. Her eldest's features appeared stonelike as he carried a basket loaded with squash, cucumbers, and purple carrots toward the house. He moved so close, Calah shrank back while Cain bumped into his brother until Abel staggered. Vegetables spilled over from either side of the basket, but Cain didn't stop. Nor did he pick up the fallen produce. Abel rubbed his shoulder, his features drawn.

Was the action on Cain's part intentional? Surely not. Surely Cain wouldn't do something so vindictive. He would apologize to Abel later. If not, she would ask Cain to make things right once he cooled.

"Cain needs a wife of his own. Edina must be his choice," Eve said as she reached for her husband, slipping her hand into the crook of his arm for comfort. "It might tame the storm brewing in him."

But as soon as she uttered her observation, loud fighting erupted from inside the house where Edina sewed, Cain's shouts echoing throughout the field and orchard. Moments later, Edina stormed from the house, her fists balled at her side. Cain was nowhere to be seen.

"Why do you stand outside gawking? Are your ears burning from eavesdropping?" Edina yelled at her siblings.

Abel held up a warning hand, but Calah stretched her full height, her tone stern. "You two chased away the birds with your hollering."

With a growl, Edina fled into the field while Abel and Calah whispered to each other.

"No woman can save a man," Adam finally said, his tone cryptic. "Cain has too much anger in him to be of any benefit to either Edina or Calah."

"Don't say such things," Eve protested. "He needs us. He needs a family of his own. We can't leave him alone. You know more than anyone that it isn't good to be alone."

Adam disentangled from her grip, and she bit the inside of her cheek to avoid saying more, lest she repeat the argument of old and hear Adam's accusations of her coddling their eldest.

"One thing is for certain. He cannot lead our family when I'm gone, Eve. He doesn't have the self-control or the wisdom. Now, Abel—"

"Is a dutiful son. The son you always wanted," she interrupted, "yes, I know Abel is the better choice to lead our family. But perhaps you can talk with Cain and smooth the way and get him to see Edina in a different light. She has always traipsed after him, even as a child. Maybe she can help Cain, if given enough opportunity. If only Cain would see her worth…"

Adam didn't answer her, but she couldn't help but note how haggard he looked. A touch of white, a single strand, gleamed from his temple. He was aging, even if little by little.

Eve remained in the orchard, plucking what ripe fruit she could while her husband took the beaten path far from the house, leaving Cain ultimately alone to stew in his anger.

Yes, she knew what her eldest wanted. He wanted Calah, and Calah remained as elusive and remote as ever to him, while Edina sat fuming and rejected.

Was it possible Cain gravitated to the things he couldn't have?

Guilt suffused Eve, bringing an acidic taste to her mouth. Why must she see the mistakes of her past repeated in her children, over and over?

She knew the answer to that question, but knowing the answer didn't bring any comfort. Her sin had done this to Cain. To Edina. To Calah and to Abel. And she would never escape the consequences of it.

The fragrant plums demanded Eve's attention, almost too squishy to the touch, and she dared not risk losing the latest crop. Despite the urgency of the tasks waiting to be completed, she couldn't quite shake the need to confront Cain. Truthfully, Adam needed to speak to his firstborn, though her husband had disappeared into his flock, no doubt finding solace with his precious animals.

Must he leave her with the dreaded task? Would Adam reveal his decision not to make Cain the next leader? Eve's pulse raced at the idea of yet more conflict.

The house loomed in the distance, now quiet. Abel had taken Calah's hand, leading her farther away from the house, near a private copse of trees. No longer did they laugh and jest, but Abel's arm had stolen around Calah's shoulders, drawing her close enough to kiss.

If there was a time to speak to Cain, it was now. Eve sucked in a breath through her teeth.

Why then did her feet feel as though they were mired in the loose soil, preventing her from taking another step?

Instead, she left her basket under the plum tree and searched for Edina to offer what comfort she could.

Tensions strained later that evening when the men sat down with Eve and her daughters around the fire. Without a word or a smile, Calah passed out bowls of roasted nuts and fruit. Edina brought in a wooden platter of eggs and vegetables, equally silent.

Calah kept her head down, her brown hair obscuring her delicate features, while Cain tracked her slightest movements. On the opposite end of the mat, Edina's eyes remained red and swollen from weeping in the garden. She tossed her black hair over her shoulders and sniffed loudly, but Cain didn't seem to notice.

But the memory of her weeping lingered with Eve, breaking Eve's heart as she recalled her daughter's desperation.

"I will be alone, Mama. Forever. No one wants me. Abel and Calah are so close. I've wanted the same with Cain, and some days, he tolerates me. Sometimes, he gives me a hug or two. But I know he wants Calah. Who will take me as a wife? God at least gave you Father. He has given me no one. I'm so tired of waiting for a home of my own. I don't want to live in a crowded house, forgotten by everyone for the rest of my life."

Eve's answer, though hopeful, hadn't comforted her daughter. "You must be patient, Edina. Our Father will provide what you need. Trust Him."

Cross-legged and relaxed, Cain alone revealed no emotion while everyone spoke with exaggerated care, avoiding bringing up the earlier fight. At last, Abel cleared his throat. He shifted on his mat, nudging aside the fruit in front of him as if his appetite had fled. His eyes, however, sparkled with barely constrained excitement.

"I want to ask your blessing, Father and Mother." Abel inclined his head in Eve's direction as well. He entwined his fingers through Calah's, earning a shy smile from her as she finally raised her head, her eyes shining like the stars at night.

"Calah and I have spoken with each other, and we want to start a home of our own—with your permission, of course."

Silence fell in the room, and Abel's expression dimmed.

"You have my blessing," Adam finally spoke, his voice thick with emotion. "May God grant you many, many children."

Eve felt a flush hit her cheeks. She had wanted far more children than she had been given. Why had God commanded her to fill the earth and then denied her womb?

Calah reached out and touched Eve's arm. "Mama, I won't leave you. We've decided to live close to you and Father, even if Abel wants to build a home of his own."

Eve patted her daughter's hand. "I'm grateful you'll be close. Having you and your children near will bring me much comfort in the seasons to come. At least I'll have plenty of babies to snuggle and play with."

A side glance in Cain's direction revealed her eldest's neck. A muscle jumped near his lean jawline.

If Adam noticed his eldest's tension, he gave no sign. "We've much to celebrate. I think this calls for a special sacrifice, to ask for God's direction and provision."

"No." The answer ground out of Cain, shocking and vehement.

Abel didn't flinch. If anything, he leaned forward, demonstrating his resolve. "It isn't up to you."

"No," Cain repeated a second time, his voice like a hiss. He jabbed at his chest with a rigid thumb. "I am the eldest. I should have the first choice in marriage. I should be the first one to be given a wife. Will I not be the leader of our family one day? Why have none of you asked what I want?"

Adam raised both palms up to calm the tension. "The decision has been made, Cain. You must respect it, regardless of how you feel. I have allowed Abel and Calah to decide their partnering, and they both agreed to join with each other. Be at peace and rejoice with your brother. Tomorrow, we will seek God as we have these past seasons. You, Abel, and I will each offer our own sacrifice. Perhaps God will reveal what plan He has for you, if you will listen."

Cain jumped up and yanked aside the screen before vanishing into the night. With an inarticulate noise, Edina rose from the mat and hurried after her brother.

"I've hurt him," Abel said. He rubbed his chest as if Cain had struck it. "I never meant to. Please believe me. It seems nothing I do satisfies my brother."

"He had dreams of his own," Eve hurried to explain, stuttering over her words in her haste to console. "But after tonight, he must accept what has happened and discover a new path. Besides, we all know how close you and Calah have been over the years. It's hardly surprising that the two of you would wish for a home of your own."

Calah nodded as she folded her arms tight across her middle. "Cain asked me a season ago, and I refused. I-I didn't want to be his wife."

Eve sank back onto the mat in shock. How had she missed so much in her family?

Later that night, she sought the comfort of the outdoors, where the stars glittered bright and cold in the sky. Shivering in the damp air, she studied the flickering planets and the milky stretch rippling through the heavens. Would her Father intervene? He had proven faithful, even if silent.

A familiar presence brushed against her shoulder. Adam's low voice claimed her attention. "You are troubled with Abel's decision."

How well her husband knew her.

She weighed her thoughts carefully before speaking. "I'm not entirely pleased. Part of me had hoped Father would create other men and women from ribs, just as He had made me for you. This—this situation feels far too difficult for our children to navigate, each one forced to choose between each other. If only Cain wanted Edina. It would make life so much easier. If only there was someone else waiting for him and for Edina. But I know our children need to partner. No one can survive the wilderness alone. We need children. We need each other."

Adam gave an aggrieved nod. "I suspect it will be a choice, perhaps only for our family at this particular moment. It won't always have to be this way, Eve. I pleaded too, for God to make partners for our offspring, but somehow, I think, by the time Abel and Cain have children, and their children have children, it won't be so difficult. Nor so intense a choice."

She highly doubted it, judging by the fleeting but heated expressions she had just witnessed over the previous meal. God had given her to Adam, and their union had proved far more challenging than she would have cared for. But Adam wasn't entirely wrong. The ewes had sheep every year. The rabbits proliferated in the forest, providing plenty of food for the wolves. Each animal kind continued to multiply and spread until the meadow Adam had claimed was teeming with life.

A minor consolation to the suffering of her children.

Cain's bitter disappointment brought an equally bitter taste to her mouth. When had her eldest reached out to Calah? Her daughter had not said one word until this evening.

Had Cain pressured Calah? Did Calah no longer trust Eve enough to share each detail, each worry? Was it wrong to want to be involved in her children's choices?

A cramp in Eve's abdomen made her stumble. A sickening dread brought the acidic taste back to her mouth and the pounding headache at her temples. She clapped her hand over her lips before she could stop herself.

"You are not well." Adam wrapped a hard arm around her waist—an action that steadied her and brought a measure of comfort. "You should rest, Eve."

Biting her lip, she nodded.

Truthfully, she couldn't take any more conflict. Nor loss.

CHAPTER TWENTY

Eve heard when Cain crept into the house in the wee hours of the night. She had half expected him to bolt and disappear for days, considering his angst during the evening meal. She pulled back the leather drape separating her and Adam from the main room and watched as her eldest set a spear on the floor and stretched out his long form on a mat near the opening. Calah and Edina slept behind another partition, the additional leather panels acting as dividers between the main living space.

Perhaps it was best Abel slept with his sheep this evening, an action Adam readily approved. The larger the flock, the more care required, forcing both Adam and Abel to spend nights outside, guarding with spears. Especially since the house felt unbearably suffocating with anger hidden beneath false smiles and muttered whispers.

Cain despised the sheep, claiming they made him smell. He would always be her gardener, preferring the scent of plants, flowers, and earth. She watched him a moment longer, waiting for the rhythmic sound of deep sleep.

Her eldest would be fine. He always found a way back to her. Yet the usual assurances felt stretched far too thin to be of any comfort.

She settled into her mat while Adam's deep, even breaths encouraged her to relax.

Edina had also returned home, albeit before Cain, dry-eyed and with a curious smile curving her lips. Just what had happened between those two? Had Cain decided Edina would make a good wife after all? Had he found a measure of peace and wisdom in accepting Adam's declaration?

A more troubling thought stole any vestiges of sleep. She would be alone again, except for this new baby. And though she was grateful that her children would have a future, a sense of being left behind, of no longer being needed, brought a renewed restlessness to her spirit.

Adam rolled over, mumbling in his sleep. She burrowed into her husband's side and savored what companionship she could.

Sunlight peeked through the roof, sliding golden rays along the mud-brick walls. Eve squinted and pushed up from her mat, the woven reeds crinkling beneath her hand. Her husband's familiar form no longer lay beside her. When she brushed aside the curtain, no one else remained in the house. Her daughters had risen before her. And here she lay about with a weariness in her bones. The baby wiggled within her as if to agree.

She wanted nothing more than to sleep, but today, Adam would offer sacrifices on behalf of their family. There would be many discussions in the days to come. How to divide the land. Where to build a new house for the new couple.

Perhaps having more room wouldn't be such a terrible idea, especially with another baby coming.

Nervousness and delight warred within Eve, but beneath the conflicted feelings, her heart thudded with increasing unease as she reconsidered the events of the previous day. Abel's bright-eyed declarations, Calah's shy acceptance, and Cain's harsh denial of the upcoming partnership with Abel and Calah becoming as one.

Dare she hope Cain finally found peace with Edina?

She quickly braided her hair, a technique she'd learned from making the baskets, and captured the ends of the long strands with a rawhide string. The morning light glinted off a silver strand—just a single strand peeking from the purest black. What did it mean? She plucked it from her head and swiftly discarded it. Surely it was nothing to fret over—one mere gray hair.

The urgency to set things right with her family intensified. Flipping the braid over her shoulder, she secured a belt around her tunic, her stomach rounding like the peaches in her orchard. As Eve headed to the orchard, she waved at Edina, who was removing tanned skins from the racks positioned near the house.

"It's a beautiful day, Mama!" Edina cupped her hand over her mouth to yell.

Eve chuckled at her daughter, who beamed, her movements graceful and lilting, almost like the mating dance of a paradise bird. Yes, something wonderful must have happened late at night to make Edina grin. Cain had finally come to his senses and realized Edina was more than enough of a match for him. Otherwise, he would have to wait. One thing was for certain—Cain was not good at waiting.

Thank You, Father. Thank You for answering me. Edina needs a husband. She needs love as much as I do.

It hit her then, how lonely her daughter must feel—the same feeling Eve had wrestled with for so many moons. She would spend more time with Edina and less in the garden. More with Calah too, and share what she knew about being a partner to Adam. There were delicate things a young woman needed to know once she was mature enough to handle the truth.

Yet these thoughts scattered from Eve's mind when she entered the orchard. There, Cain stood in a clearing between the trees, his piercing gaze pinned on Calah, who spoke so softly that the wind snatched her words.

But Eve saw enough.

"You must give me another chance, Calah. I want to be with you and you alone," Cain all but groaned as he reached for her, his grip tight on her shoulders. With one smooth motion, he yanked her against his chest, ignoring her squeak of protest. Calah swung her leg back and kicked him in his shin, earning a howl from Cain.

"I said no!" Calah's voice rose shrilly. She pivoted on her heel and ran out of the orchard, past Eve, who remained stunned.

Her eldest flinched when he spied Eve at the edge of the orchard.

"Cain—" She moved forward to speak with him, but he too turned as if to escape the confining row of trees and her probing questions.

"Cain!"

He sighed and rolled his neck and shoulders as if to release trapped tension, yet pain marked the planes of his hard mouth. "Yes, I heard you the first time."

"I—I had hoped—" Her throat burned as did her cheeks. Oh, what a conversation to have as a mother! She stammered out the rest. "I thought you and Edina had come to some sort of understanding."

He immediately squared his shoulders, his eyes darkening as he studied her. "Why? Did she say something to you?"

Eve's mouth dried as she stared at her eldest, who now seemed more unfathomable, as if she had never raised him. "No, not exactly. She just seemed in such a good mood this morning, I assumed you finally chose her. I saw her enter the house late at night, just before you entered."

Instead of being mortified, a harsh laugh escaped Cain. "Is that all you saw, Mama? Edina slinking home?"

"What happened last night, Cain?"

He muttered something. Something that felt foul, and yet it was too low for her to discern.

When she raised her eyebrows, he expelled an exasperated breath. "Nothing, nothing to worry about."

"You must let Calah go. She will partner with Abel. Your father has spoken, and that is an end to it. If I were you, I'd spend more time preparing a sacrifice than chasing after what you cannot have."

The look he cast in her direction made her shudder. When had her sweet son, her darling boy, become something so—so...

She didn't want to think of the white serpent and its long, writhing form, squeezing around the Tree of Knowledge of Good and Evil.

Cain was not truly bad. He couldn't be. He was simply misguided, and he needed firm but gentle instruction to set him on the right path.

She clutched her basket close to her chest while an ache throbbed inside of her, not unlike all those years ago when she had experienced birthing pains with Cain. "Make yourself useful to your father. And stay away from Calah."

When she stood alone in the orchard, a poor and dismal imitation of Eden, she dashed away her tears with shaking hands. In the seasons that had passed, she had not encountered the white serpent again. But sometimes, during the darkest hour of the night, or when she or her family fought, she felt his presence as if he sat cross-legged, warming himself by her fire.

When she plucked the nearest peach, her grip so tight, she pierced the fuzzy skin until juice dripped into her palm, the terrifying sensation of being watched returned, reminding her it was more than just her imagination.

And the prickle rippling across her skin warned of something lurking at the edge of the orchard—something that felt cold and dangerous, wicked and hungry.

By the time the sun moved west, signaling the middle part of the day, Eve had collected her fruit and returned to the house to store her supplies. She saw no sign of Edina or the leather skins drying outside. Inside, the circular house remained empty, with no sounds of rustling or giggles or chatter. She set her basket down but not before she spied an unusual string on Calah's mat. Eve reached down and picked up the rawhide knotted at various points with shells in between. Tiny, pearlescent shells with hints of green and white flecked across a glossy surface.

It was a gift. Not unlike the rare flowers Adam found for her.

Carefully, she tucked it beneath a leather skin covering the mat, so as not to be disturbed.

Who had given Calah such a carefully designed piece? It was not practical like clothing. But it was meant to be worn, perhaps around a neck or an arm or an ankle, and enhance the wearer's beauty. Had Abel made the decoration for his sister?

Voices reverberated outside, the shouts of men breaking the silence. Eve hurried outside to see her second son bring forth one of the prized lambs from the stone-walled pens where other lambs bleated their protests.

It was perfect, with nary a blemish or spot on its wool. So white and clean, it resembled the lazy clouds floating above in the blue sky. He held the lamb with such reverence that it brought a wistful smile to Eve. With her son's black hair tousled by the wind and his green eyes shining, how happy he looked.

Unfortunately, Cain was nowhere to be seen. Would he bring a sacrifice, as Adam had declared the night prior?

She closed the distance between herself and Abel, the dirt swirling beneath the soles of her feet. "You've chosen the very best, haven't you, Abel?" She reached out to caress the small lamb.

He nodded, and to her surprise, his eyes suddenly welled with tears. "It's for Him. For all He has done for me."

"For you?" Eve paused to study her son.

"I want to thank God. I want Him to know how much I love Him and how much I need Him. Look at all the blessings He has given me. My family and Calah. He has gifted me with life and health and the animals I love so much. How could I not worship at His feet?"

She kept quiet as her son continued, "I need His guidance, especially as Calah and I start our family. This lamb—it's as Father said so many seasons ago—I need an atonement for all the wrong things I've done in my life. For all the times I've hurt my family and God. I want to be right with Him, Mama. I know I can't be good on my own. I've tried. But we need so much more help than what we can muster, don't we? We need God's mercy and forgiveness."

"God did intervene," Eve agreed. "He killed animals to cover my shame and your father's. Ever since then, your father has wanted to offer sacrifices. There is always a cost to sin. I have always regretted what happened at the forbidden tree. I felt as though I destroyed everyone I loved, including this world. If I could take it all back, I would. It's strange to think something so innocent as this lamb should be the one that pays the cost for what we've done."

Abel eyed the worn path leading to the altar, but when he turned back to regard her, his smile comforted. "Yes, it doesn't seem quite fair, does it? A sweet lamb taking our sins. But He promised to send a deliverer for us, and He clothed you, Mama, even in your moment of nakedness. He will make a way for each of us to return to Him, even if Eden remains closed. We have to choose to follow Him no matter what happens. We have to trust Him, regardless of what life brings."

She withdrew her hand from the lamb, the moment bittersweet, knowing what would happen next to the animal so safe in her son's arms. "How well you remember my stories, and you were so tiny when I first told you of Eden. If only Cain listened half as well as you."

Abel leaned close enough to kiss her on the cheek while keeping a firm grip on the lamb. "One day, I will tell my children the same stories you told me."

Before she could say anything more, he left with the lamb to prepare it for sacrifice. Blinking, she could only touch her cheek.

Three altars waited near the edge of the meadow. One old and stained from use, the other two recent additions with carefully placed rocks smeared with fresh mud. It was a momentous occasion, marking Adam's children following in obedience.

Eve and her daughters approached the altars, waiting for Adam and her sons to arrive with their sacrifices. As the sun turned golden and deep, coating everything with mellow hues, she wrapped one arm around Calah and the other around Edina, despite their age, and drew them close. Calah rubbed her arms as if she might ward against a chill despite the balmy weather. Edina no longer had a smile softening her features. They leaned into her just as they did when they barely reached her knee.

"How much longer before Father comes?" Edina finally wiggled free of Eve's embrace. She brushed aside her loose hair with shaking fingers, tucking a wave behind her ear.

Compassion flooded Eve as she regarded her daughter's pensive expression. "Any moment now." Whatever previous joy had sparkled within Edina had now fled. Had Cain had taken out his frustration on her?

Another dreaded conversation to have.

But before Eve could ask questions, Calah cried out when she spotted Adam and Abel carrying the lambs to the altars. Their somber expressions mirrored how Eve felt. This was a sacred moment. A holy moment. Adam normally took responsibilities for the sacrifices, but in encouraging his sons to take leadership, he would ensure the practice would be passed down to the next generation.

Abel brought the lamb, tied at the hooves, and placed it on top of his altar. He paused, as if uncertain, his glance toward Adam full of unspoken questions.

"We will wait for Cain." Adam's tight answer stirred even more tension in the group.

There was no sign of their eldest. Not in the copse of trees lining the meadow, nor in the enclosed field or the garden. They waited. Meanwhile, the sun slipped into the horizon, flaming orange and threatening to fully descend.

"We cannot wait," Adam finally spoke. "We will sacrifice to God before nightfall."

Her husband sounded weary. Sad. With a resigned sigh, he gestured to Abel to continue. Abel withdrew his sharpened bone and raised his fist high above the lamb when Edina cried out.

Eve turned to see Cain running with his arms laden with produce. He huffed as he reached his altar, dropping a peach from the bounty in his arms. Without explanation, he dumped his assortments of vegetables and fruit onto his platform. A melon, carrots, leafy greens, grains with the long stems, and plums lay haphazardly in a small pile.

He wiped his filthy hands onto his tunic, sniffing loudly as he belligerently stared at Adam, then Abel, as if to defy them.

Eve cried out, unable to contain her dismay. Had Cain just picked the vegetables as an afterthought? Was this a joke? Or an insult? Her eldest avoided her gaze, and that of Edina's and Calah's.

"You should have brought a lamb," Abel said with a frown as he regarded his brother's sacrifice.

At once, Cain's demeanor changed into something savage. "Why? Why should we kill a perfectly good animal? It's cruel, and I can't believe God would demand something so horrible to honor Him. Why must you spill blood to talk to God? How can you not be bothered by such actions?"

Eve shifted on the soft dirt, uncomfortable with such a harsh question, but it was one she had challenged Adam with years ago. To her surprise, her husband appeared as stunned as she. He opened his mouth and shut it. Yet he did not argue with Cain. A strange thing, since Adam had argued with Eve all those years ago when she had challenged him about animal sacrifice.

"Sin should disturb us," Abel spoke first. "I never said killing a lamb didn't hurt me. Believe me, I hate it, perhaps more than anyone. I raised these lambs, took care of them when they were ill, and watched over them to ensure they were well fed. But it is what our father has taught us, and it represents what God did in the garden when He clothed our parents."

The words rang within Eve, lighting a spark. *"Sin should disturb us."* She remembered Adam's reaction, when he nearly threw up after seeing the first animal skins spread across the grass.

Oh, the consequences she faced because of her disobedience. Every day she dealt with it. Yet sin also had a numbing effect. It became almost normal and expected.

"I will no longer walk with you," her Father had warned. She had spent the rest of her days longing to be with Him again, yet helpless against the pull of her actions and thoughts and desires. Abel answered Cain so much better than she could have. The first time her eldest had complained about the sacrifices, she had held her tongue. Unlike her and Adam, Abel chose boldness.

"I'm not getting another lamb," Cain said through his teeth. "I've brought the best of the crops. Can't you see the work of my hands? This is who I am. This is what I do, and I've given my very best to God. Surely you can't argue with that, Father? I'm late because I searched everywhere in our fields and garden for the choicest vegetables and fruits. If God made these plants, then surely He will be pleased with my offering."

Adam's throat bobbed as his gaze flitted between both altars and both of his sons. "We cannot wait. Let us approach God."

Whatever protest lodged in Eve's throat died at Adam's ready acquiescence.

Cain approached his altar and tilted his head once in quick deference, but not before Eve spied his triumphant smile. Her eldest did not remain bowed for long. He withdrew his flint rocks from the satchel that hung about his neck. The sound of the rocks striking each other echoed across the meadow.

Abel, however, remained before his platform with his head bowed. Eve felt a curious pull toward her younger son. Before she realized, she had reached her younger son's side.

"We should be disturbed by sin."

What if Abel was the intended deliverer? She gasped as the thought sunk into her, but it refused to let go. Abel's arm descended in a flash, holding the bone instrument before it plunged into the innocent lamb. Speaking out loud, he begged God to forgive each of their sins. Smoke soon billowed, rising to the heavens, as both men lit their sacrifices. Cain's damp vegetables hissed and sputtered, the flames dying as quickly as they began, but Abel offered his lamb, even the fat portions, giving the very best and saving nothing for himself.

A roaring fire consumed Abel's sacrifice, until at last, the smell of burnt meat and ash clung to the humid air.

Abel blinked away the wetness in his eyes. Eve's heart lurched as she bowed her head along with her younger son. A swift side glance revealed Calah lowering her head in deference to the Creator.

Edina, however, remained next to Cain, who, with his chin raised high, stared at the blackened ruins of his fruit. He folded his brawny arms across his chest, his posture rigid. Yet Eve could have sworn that she witnessed confusion in her eldest.

Had he truly thought God would be pleased?

Twilight descended as Eve and two of her children returned home. She felt something momentous had occurred. Perhaps they all did. Cain remained next to his altar, poking at the blackened remains of the peaches and plums and withered greens. He said nothing, but something in him appeared to harden, judging from his expression. Edina remained next to him, unusually silent as she fidgeted with her braid. She made no move to follow Eve home.

With a sigh, Eve left the two of them in the dusky evening. An ache in her belly hastened her steps, urging her to find a mat soon. But any worry was chased away when she saw Abel reach for Calah's hand, entwining his fingers with hers. The sight made Eve grin, reminding her of Adam in the garden of Eden.

"I asked God for His blessing on our union," he told Calah, swinging her hand in his, the action tender and almost carefree.

"I asked as well," Calah answered, no longer sounding as shy. "And I asked for children of our own. Plenty of babies with dimples in their cheeks just like yours."

Together, they hurried down the beaten path, moving farther and farther from Adam and Eve. But only peace filled Eve's heart as she watched her children together. Calah's light laughter caught in the breeze when Abel ducked his head to whisper something in her ear.

Eve felt a familiar hand on her shoulder. She glanced up just in time to catch Adam's smile. "Abel offered his very best this day. I couldn't be more proud of our son. He is the one who will lead our family when I am gone," he said.

"I thought the same as you," she admitted readily. "I had even wondered if Abel might be the promised deliverer when I saw him at the altar. If so, the idea brings my heart much hope. I felt as though God heard Abel's prayer and blessed our youngest son's offering. As for Cain, something felt not right." She let her words trail, still concerned over her eldest's demeanor.

"Yes," Adam agreed slowly. "His suggestion of a crop to be used as a sacrifice surprised me, and for a moment, I wondered if perhaps I might be wrong in offering only animals, but then, the longer I thought about it, the more the idea troubled me. Do we have the right to tell God how we will approach Him? I don't think so. Abel has displayed a rare wisdom, more than any of our other children. Or us, for that matter."

Neither she nor Adam said Cain's name. In fact, Adam had kept his voice quiet, but a prickle across Eve's shoulders made her glance behind. There, in the gathering shadows, marched Cain with his face unreadable in the gloom of the night. Edina trudged behind her brother, with her head downcast and her hair falling forward to obscure her features.

Another inarticulate sound escaped Eve, and her husband's hand tightened on her shoulder in response.

Just how much had Cain heard?

CHAPTER TWENTY-ONE

A rooster crowed, signaling the early dawn. Bleary-eyed, Eve staggered from her pallet, fully determined to tend to her garden. But a fresh stab in her abdomen reduced her to weaving baskets inside the cave. Adam had opened a section of the roof at night so that the sprinkle of white stars would distract her from the growing discomfort. Both of them remembered the pain of her first delivery and feared a reoccurrence of miscarriage. At least she could glimpse at the blue sky above and see the clouds float past.

Before he left for the animal pen, Adam kissed her forehead and fussed over her, refusing to let her even walk across the room to retrieve her basket of supplies and her collection of loose reeds. After dropping the berry-stained reeds and grass into her hands, an assortment of deep blue and red strands now dried, he made her promise she wouldn't attempt too much in the fields.

"Someone has to make the evening meal," she protested, dismayed by the thought of remaining indoors for the entire day.

He waggled a finger at her. A hint of a smile took the edge from his warning. "You have two grown daughters who are more than capable of cooking or any other errands. I don't want you going through another delivery like the first."

"Walking takes the edge from the labor," she reminded him.

"Fine. Walk as you need," he agreed, "But allow Calah and Edina to actually assist you with the household work."

She was about to protest when he coughed suddenly and rubbed his chest with his fist.

"What's wrong? Are you sick?"

"No," he said thickly. "It's nothing more than a tickle in the back of my throat. I'm just thirsty." But the beads of sweat clinging to his forehead said otherwise.

He reached out and fingered a strand of her hair. "Please, Eve, for my sake. I have more than enough to worry about."

How could she argue with such a plea? The memory of that awful first delivery would forever be seared into her.

She nodded as she reached for the nearest dyed strands of dried grass. The morning wasn't entirely unpleasant. With the door open, she caught glimpses of the activity outside. Calah came to bring her fruit near the midday point.

But as the heat sweltered, Eve wished she could take back her promise and head out to her garden to dig and haul baskets where the plants offered shade and the wind somewhat of a breeze to cool her flushed skin. She was about to leave when Edina joined her on the mat.

"Mama, Cain is worried about the crops. He asked me to come to you for advice."

Eve paused as she inserted the grass into the nearest loop of the basket taking form. "What do you mean?"

"The black blight returned. Almost overnight, it seemed. Have you ever seen something spread this quickly in your life? I told him perhaps God was angry about the sacrifice, but

Cain…" Edina's bottom lip trembled as she folded her hands across her lap. "He wouldn't hear anything of it. He blames the rest of us for not listening to him. He said you and Father should have given him more time to prepare."

"And it's our fault?" Eve could scarcely believe what she was hearing. If Cain hadn't spent his morning pestering Calah, he might have found the right lamb and brought a proper offering. Why couldn't he simply take responsibility for his behavior instead of blaming others, including her?

"He said you've always favored Abel. Now God is favoring Abel over him."

Eve inhaled deeply to control her rising temper. Nothing could be further from the truth. She had not favored Abel. Adam, yes, had favored their younger son. But not Eve. If anything, she had tried to show her eldest how much she loved him, how much she understood him, and how much she wished only the best for him.

"What of this blight? Can he not cut the few bad stalks and burn them?"

Edina paused, her hands twisting the edge of her frayed belt. "Mama, it's the entire crop."

The blight that she had asked God to remove had returned with a vengeance. The field in front of Eve, with each row recently weeded, should have been the picture of health. Today, even from her position near the rock wall, she didn't even need to venture into the first row to see the extent of the damage. Entire stalks of grain had blackened, as if covered with mold. Nothing remained untouched, including the clusters of peas and the pumpkins with trailing vines, with leaves now withering to a sickly brown.

A groan escaped her as she braced one palm against the wall.

Everything gone.

Edina brushed against Eve's shoulder. "See? It's not good. I don't know if we can save much. I pulled out a few of the carrots and they appeared fine, but they are too small to feed our entire family."

Eve struggled to speak as she stared at the ruined field. A lean season, one of hunger and desperation, might return yet again. There simply wasn't enough food for everyone. The ache in her belly intensified, jabbing and sharp. What would she tell Adam? The season had passed, and though they might plant more squash, they would take far too long to grow.

She dreaded adding to his already insurmountable burden.

As she scanned the field, one absence loomed. "Where is Cain?"

"He left for the river to wash." Edina wrapped her arm around Eve's shoulder. "Is this blight because of Cain's sacrifice? Did he anger God?"

Eve enfolded her daughter in an embrace and ignored the pain in her abdomen. She would not lose another child. *She would not.*

Her answer, however, sounded frail. "I don't know."

But perhaps she or Adam should have said something and stopped Cain. Perhaps…

If only she could hear her Father's voice and glean from His wisdom. Surely she could use some of it now with her family.

"Come with me," Eve told her husband as he stood at the edge of the meadow, watching over his flock.

His eyebrows shot upward when he saw her wade through the long grass and wildflowers to reach his side. "The crops are likely destroyed."

He immediately left Abel with the sheep and followed her back to the stone wall enclosing the field. She walked with him down the rows, pausing only to examine the ruined leaves.

"I don't think I have ever seen something move this fast," Adam said as he rubbed his chin.

Eve had. The day she fled Eden, she had witnessed the effects of her choice ripple outward like rings on a pond, ruining both field and stream and anything else in its path.

"What will we do?" she asked.

He frowned as his hand dropped to his chest and lingered there as if something hurt him. "We have enough livestock to provide milk and eggs. We'll burn what's lost and start over again if need be."

"Can we survive on what is left?"

He glanced down at her, his mouth pressed into a firm line before he answered. "We'll have to."

When they returned to the house, Cain carried two limp fish dangling at the end of his spear.

"You saw the garden?" Cain rasped as he slid one gray fish from the spear and then the other. He set his spear against the wall of the house, keeping his gaze averted.

"I see no choice but to burn the crop. Edina thinks we can rescue some root vegetables underground such as the carrots, but as for the rest…" Adam's tone remained grim as he folded his arms across his chest. "I expect you to handle the burning. I've got too much to do today with the herd."

Cain did not reply, and nor did Adam stay. Both men passed each other, so close and yet so distant.

Eve waited, however, while her son laid the fish on a clean frond and removed his tools to gut the silvery flesh. She remained silent while he sliced into the scales, removing the largest of the bones.

"What are you doing with those fish?" she finally dared to ask.

"I'm going to eat them, Mama. What does it look like?"

Revulsion roiled within her. "We eat only what is grown, Cain. Not what moves."

He hummed under his breath. "I don't think that will work with the fields ruined. Months ago, I saw a bear catching fish downstream, far beyond our homestead. If it can eat fish, why can't I?"

"God told us to eat the plants and the seeds."

"Why, Mama? If the fish tastes good and nourishes me, why can't I? Why must I deny myself?"

She had no answer for that, her soul troubled by his belligerent declaration. Cain's experienced movements slicing into the gleaming scales suggested this wasn't his first killing. In the past, her family had hunted for skins but never for flesh. When had Cain changed?

"How did God sound when He spoke to you?" Cain's question further rattled Eve. Of all the comments or complaints she expected to hear from her son, this was not one of them.

"His voice was majestic. I don't know how to describe it, but when I heard Him bid me to awaken, I felt so much joy, peace, and excitement."

Cain nudged the fillets into the wide frond. She couldn't help but notice how his fingers shook as he clenched the tool.

"I heard Him," he finally admitted. His clear eyes bore into hers as hard as the cave walls. "This morning, by the river."

Despite the dismay of the morning, a sliver of excitement mixed with sharp longing pierced her. She sat down on the ground, cradling her belly. "Cain! That is wonderful. I have not heard His voice in so long. What did He say to you?"

Her eldest wiped his tools on the grass and slid them into his pouch. "God said, 'Why are you angry? Why is your face downcast? If you do what is right, will you not be accepted? But if you do not do what is right, sin is crouching at your door; it desires to have you, but you must rule over it.'"

The wind rushed past them, stirring the grass and the leaves in the trees. In the distance, sounds of the forest barely registered in Eve's mind—the bleating of the animals, along with Abel's excited shout.

"Oh, Cain," was all she could say at first. How she had longed to hear God's voice again, to hear His encouragement. How she had longed for her children to experience the same.

But this warning brought a wave of fresh anxiety.

He laughed, the sound strangely dark and without mirth. "Are you disappointed, Mama? I shouldn't be so surprised. After all, it appears I disappoint everyone. Even God feels the need to criticize my every move."

She rubbed his back, dropping her hand when his eyes flashed like fire. "He is right. You can't have this anger roiling inside you. It will only destroy, just like the blight in our fields."

Cain growled low in his throat. "I am angry. I'm angry about many things. If He truly loved me, He would accept me just as I am. After all, didn't He make me this way? Why must I be the one who bends to His will? Why can't He bend if He is so almighty? Is He so proud that He must force us to do exactly as He pleases?"

How she longed to reach her son and to show him a better path. If only he would listen to her. But a far more chilling thought took hold. If Cain refused God's voice, then surely her son would not listen to any reason, no matter who spoke.

Such ruthless, stubborn rebellion—it was enough to steal the air out of her lungs.

Mouth dry, she tried again to move Cain. "You have come to God, telling Him how He is to accept your worship. Isn't that pride on your part? God, our heavenly Father, the Creator of the world, who is without beginning or end. The One who formed the stars and set the planets in the sky. The God who sees over the vast and the small. Do you want to advise Him on what is right and what is wrong? Your sacrifice the other night wasn't really about honoring Him. It was only about you, Cain. There is no one in your world more important than you. I saw it when you tried to force Calah to kiss you. I've seen in the way you reject Edina and treat her with so much contempt when all she wants is your affection. You have disrespected your father and now me. Oh, Cain, why? *Why* must you tear this family apart? All we want is to love you and be loved by you."

He leaped to his feet, a vein nearly popping at his temple. "How dare you! How dare you speak to me in such a way. You, Mama, who broke the world, passing judgment on me. If anyone should be made to suffer, it's *you*."

Tears slid down her cheeks, hot and salty. She did not brush them aside. "Please, Cain, I know I brought sin into the world. If I could take it all back, I would. I will carry this regret with me for as long as I live. I will never forgive myself, and I dare not ask it of others. Please believe me. I don't want you to suffer the way I have. You are my precious boy, my eldest. God loves you too."

"Bah!" Her son batted away her suggestion as if it were nothing more than an annoying gnat. "If this world is a demonstration of His love, then I want nothing of it."

Cain stalked past her, heading toward the fields filled with ruin. Eve returned to her mat inside the house and curled into herself, alone and weary. So very alone.

What do I do, Father? How do I reach my family?

Only silence answered her.

CHAPTER TWENTY-TWO

The dreadful rooster crowed at the break of dawn, forcing Eve to awaken from a dreamless sleep. She rubbed her bleary eyes while sitting. Adam snored beside her with his arm flung behind his head, his chest rising and falling. She hadn't had the heart to wake him yet. He never slept beyond the rising dawn, but last night had been marked with much tossing and turning and heavy sighs. More troubling, that cough continued to plague him.

Was he ill?

She crept past the sleeping forms of her family. Abel, however, must have awakened first, since his mat was empty.

The scent of acrid smoke greeted her as soon as she left the house, chasing away the pesky mosquitoes and flies. Despite the purple dawn, the enclosed field glowed red, the heat reaching her where she stood. A man faced the fire with his back to her, keeping guard over the field. She recognized Abel's stocky build. Despite having to watch over the livestock, he had risen earlier than anyone to purge the fields of the blight. A job that should have been Cain's responsibility.

Eve watched from her vantage point, bemused, as she observed her younger son. How strong he was. How unassuming. Never asking for more than what he was given.

Thank You, Father, for the gift of Abel. I fear I do not deserve such a son.

Someone draped an extra skin over her shoulders, startling her from her reverie. She glanced to see Edina standing beside her.

"Why didn't God heal the plants as He did before?" Edina asked as she shivered beneath her mantle.

A difficult question to answer.

"It's up to Him to decide when, or if, He will heal," Eve said as she tugged her shawl closer to her neck to ward off the damp air. "How can any of us tell Him what to do?"

Of course, Cain had no desire to bend his will to anyone. But Edina's next comment threw Eve off balance even more.

"Cain says I may stay with him. In return, I've also asked him to build a house close to yours, and he has agreed to my terms."

Dare Eve hope her daughter find some measure of happiness? Or would Cain merely use Edina and vent his frustrations on her? Not so long ago, she had hoped Cain would find his home with Edina. But now? Dismay filled her at the thought.

"Who else is out there for me, Mama? I have no other choice. Besides…" Edina's voice turned wistful as she continued, "it's what I've always wanted. I'll make him a good wife, and he'll grow to appreciate me more in the days to come. If he had a son of his own, he might not feel so restless."

Eve reached for her daughter's hand and squeezed it. "You will always have a home with me. I want you to be happy, but I'm no longer certain you will find peace or happiness with him. I saw him in the garden with Calah the other day. No matter who enters his life, I don't think he'll ever be content."

Edina pulled her hand free. "Don't say it. I don't want to hear another word bad about him. Cain already explained to me that he only wanted to congratulate Calah. She had the audacity to kick him. Kick him, Mama! Did you see the bruise on his shin?"

"She kicked him, trying to free herself from his embrace. I saw it with my own eyes. He was pursuing her when he should have been searching for an appropriate sacrifice."

Edina jutted out her jaw, but the light in her eyes died. "He promised me a house of my own, one far bigger than what Father made for you. He said I would always belong to him."

Nausea bubbled up within Eve. "Yes. Cain would say something like that." But Edina was far too furious to catch Eve's sarcasm. She tried a gentler approach with her daughter. "Your brother is a man of many moods. It will not be easy living under his roof. I want only what is best for you."

I would rather see you alone than in a relationship fraught with angst and endless fighting.

"I will decide what is best for me," Edina muttered as she brushed past Eve and left in the orchard's direction.

Eve heaved a sigh as she entered her garden to hunt for herbs to soothe Adam's latest cough. If only she could heal her family. How helpless the feeling, to want to decide the choices for one's child and prevent a path of pain.

An uneasy peace settled over the household during the days that followed the blight. The seasons changed, bringing less sunlight. Despite the ruined crop, now since purged by Abel's fire, Eve and her daughters dug into the fields and removed what roots, squash, carrots, and onions they could find. It wasn't enough, perhaps, for a growing family, but the hens continued to lay plenty of eggs. The orchard continued to produce fruit.

They would have enough, unlike those first seasons when Cain was a boy.

Eve washed the bounty and laid them outside to dry. The carrots, with lumpy formations, one even resembling a nose, brought an unexpected giggle to Calah and Edina as they compared their findings.

"It's decided. I have the ugliest carrots." Calah held her clump high.

"I'm not so certain," Edina retorted with a wink as she plucked a misshapen squash covered in lumps. "Who cares? As long as they taste good. I'll eat about just about anything. At least we have some food to store."

Eve loved the sound of her daughters bantering with each other. Meanwhile, the baby within her kicked, as if filled with delight at the sound. She had counted the days until her next delivery, her pulse quickening with anticipation and excitement. Another child would be so good for the family. A round-cheeked baby with a toothless grin. She had dearly missed the sound of laughter, especially in light of all the conflict that had marked her family.

In the days to come, Calah and Edina would hang an assortment of roots and herbs from the ceiling of the house to further dry and remain relatively safe. Although this season, they had found additional help from an unexpected source. A stray cat had adopted them as family. Unlike the larger lions and predators that hunted in the forest, this creature remained small, reaching Eve's calves. Its spotted fur and black-tipped ears brought delight to the entire family. When it brushed against her legs, she couldn't help but chuckle. She missed the touch of an animal. Even the hens barely tolerated her presence unless she fed them.

Of course, the scent of Cain's dried fish—fish he alone insisted on eating—might have lured the cat, but the hunt for rodents kept it fat and sleek. It stayed close, and the rodents were far less, the pitter patter of their feet no longer disturbing her in the night.

The cat sniffed the vegetables on the ground and sauntered off, tail swaying as if to reject the food. Calah and Edina burst into giggles again.

"I need a cat of my own for our new home. The other night, Abel showed me where he'd like to build, next to the copse of the trees lining the orchard. We'll be close, but…," Calah began before halting.

But far enough for privacy and the chance to start a life of their own.

"It's perfect," Eve agreed. "Perhaps the cat will have a litter."

"Would you mind if Abel and I set up a tent of our own? We have enough hides. We thought it might be best to move in the next few days. I think we will be safe enough."

Eve considered the best answer. It was tempting to beg Calah to stay as close as possible, but would the proximity be healthy for her children? "It is your decision. You are free to choose as you please."

Calah beamed, but Edina grew silent. She fussed with the assortment of onions as she tied leather strings around the produce to hang later from the bundled reeds comprising the ceiling. Nor did Edina mention Cain or his plans. If anything, Cain remained far from the house most days, taking his spear and leaving for extended periods. Where he went, she did not know. He spoke less and less, so similar to Adam.

Eve assumed her eldest was in one of his moods, needing quiet. After their last heated argument, she wasn't certain what else she could say to him to change his mind about God.

But the memory of his harsh words stung, even if she feared them true. Like the chiseled point of his weapon, they had aimed straight for her heart, piercing through to the most innermost place.

"You broke the world. If anyone deserves to hurt, it's you."

She and Adam barely spoke to each other of their mistakes in Eden, or of the bluish tree, or the forbidden fruit, and who was to blame. It was simply easier not to start the argument and to brush it aside, to bury it deep and pretend the past had never happened.

But the past could not be forgotten. Two days later, following a decent meal of eggs, roasted potatoes, and carrots on spits and plenty of pleasant chatter of future dreams and plans, Cain returned home and squatted next to the crackling fire, sitting close to Eve.

Abel shifted on his mat, his arm about Calah. Edina's eyes brightened momentarily at her brother's sudden arrival until she realized Cain did not choose to sit next to her.

"I searched for Eden," he said without preamble.

Adam dropped his egg, the yellow yolk spattering against the dirt. "Did you find it?"

Cain stretched out his legs, his gaze flickering momentarily to Calah's before returning to Adam. "No. I did not."

Air rushed out of Eve's lungs at the blunt admission. "Why would you search for it? Didn't we warn you that the entrance is guarded by a flaming sword and the cherubim?"

"I wanted to see it for myself." Her eldest shrugged one shoulder. "And...I saw *nothing*. Nothing but the endless river heading east and plenty of land stretching as far as the eye can see. I followed the river, hunting and fishing along the way, but I saw no entrance into the low hills, no massive rock wall hiding your paradise."

The admission shocked her. Had God blinded Cain to the exact location? She felt a tremor ripple through Adam as he sat next to her. They had both vowed never to return to Eden. Questions regarding the location they dodged, both equally adamant to let that knowledge lie in secrecy. Neither of them would ever forget the heat of the enormous sword, nor the terrifying angels guarding the entrance.

"It is not meant to be found," Adam spoke, his voice gravelly. "God shut Eden's door forever."

"So you say," Cain challenged with a smirk as he rubbed a scrape across his weathered knuckles.

The weighted implication stifled the pleasant chatter. Even after hearing God's voice, Cain doubted her and Adam. What would it take for her child to believe God's word?

"It is a mercy you didn't find it," Eve told her son. "Only death waits at the entrance of Eden. I, for one, have no desire to test my Father's word ever again."

"Death?" Cain scoffed. "The only death I encountered was that of a wild boar. I speared it and left its carcass to rot next to the edge of a pond."

Edina scooted over to Cain and looped her arm through his, her eyes shining and wide. She mock shivered as she leaned against him. "Your adventure sounds so exciting. What else did you see?"

He tweaked a lock of her hair before launching into another story of his survival out in the wild as he tested the land and the animals and his own endurance. Finally, when the faint embers floated above the subdued fire and the dung chips turned to ash, Cain stopped talking long enough to let Edina snatch a spit of roasted vegetables and hand it to him. He took it, bestowing a melting grin upon her. "When I faced the boar, and later, a wild female elephant separated from her calf, I realized I had only myself to rely on for safety. The elephant would have crushed me if given half the chance. But I prevailed and flung my spear into her thick hide."

"You conquered an enraged female with one throw of your spear?" Abel asked, arching one black eyebrow.

"Yes." Cain jutted out his chin as he stared back at his brother.

"You killed both a boar and an elephant?" Abel repeated slowly as he reached down and picked up Cain's spear, angling it closer to the fading fire to further inspect it. "Your spear must be superior to inflict such damage."

"Or the elephant sickly and gasping her last breath," Calah mumbled.

Cain bristled. He rose from the mat and snatched the spear out of Abel's hand.

"I know what I saw," he snarled as he jabbed out a finger, pointing toward the darkness swathing the river. "I don't need you to tell me otherwise."

Predictably, the peace shattered, but no one challenged Cain further. Instead, Adam's coughing distracted everyone and Eve rose, grateful for an excuse to find her stash of dried violet petals and licorice seeds. If that failed, she had recently discovered a new white flower with a sticky slime and pungent root that aided with coughs.

Adam dutifully chewed his medicinal herbs. These days, he hardly argued with her when she handed him a plant leaf or a root.

Abel rose to his feet and extended his hand to Calah. "Good night, Father, Mama. I hope you get a good rest. Don't worry about rising for the flock. Calah and I will take care of them."

With Calah's slender fingers entwined with his, Abel smiled as he led her further into the night.

"Where are they going?" Cain demanded, the spit in his hand forgotten. He made no move to eat as he swiveled to watch his siblings leave.

Adam answered first. "They have a tent of their own. In the days to come, Abel and I will construct their new house."

Cain made an inarticulate sound, but it was loud enough for Edina to shrink into herself, and for Eve to feel a stab of concern.

Later that night, when everyone lay down to sleep, Eve pressed against her husband, wrapping her arm around his middle. His frame, so powerful and strong, usually brought a sense of security, but not tonight.

"Adam, I'm afraid." Of what exactly, she couldn't say, but the feeling persisted, demanding immediate release. Her whisper sounded unnaturally loud to her ears, and she cringed. Hopefully, neither Cain, who slept near the door, nor Edina heard her.

Adam blew out a long breath. "Eve, I am so exhausted. I cannot talk."

A cough rattled through his chest again, and she released her hold on him, sour disappointment coursing through her. Of course he needed sleep. She felt foolish for waking him when he felt so poorly. But her anxiety would not abate. Nor did she fall asleep.

CHAPTER TWENTY-THREE

Days passed, and the baby in Eve's womb seemed to dance, tiny feet or arms moving constantly to a secret rhythm. Eve loved the feel of her child within her. She placed her hands on her stomach and spoke or sang to her youngest, her heart swelling until she thought she couldn't hold anymore love.

Thank You, Father. Thank You for the gift of life. How precious is this little one in Your sight.

In these moments, all felt mostly right with the world. These small but wonderful moments of reprieve. She did not trouble Adam anymore with her concerns. Although fear followed her wherever she went, she kept it tucked deep inside and did her best to be strong and brave.

At least Adam's cough had abated and the pain in his chest was no more, but it was clear that he too desperately needed a reprieve. His cheeks increasingly sunken and his eyes bloodshot, he worked as hard as his sons, pushing himself to create new inventions, increase his flock, cultivate the land, or do whatever need struck his attention.

Rarely did his attention linger on her for long.

But before he left for work this morning, he placed a gentle hand on her stomach and chuckled as the baby wiggled beneath his palm. He flexed his fingers and tapped back, earning more movement from the baby.

"I cannot wait to meet her."

"Her?" Eve cried out with mock dismay. "I believe we have a healthy boy."

"Hmm." Adam smiled, his eyes crinkling in the corners. "I'll be happy with any child you bring into the world, Eve. But I welcome our challenge to see who will be right in the end."

She dearly hoped the new child would bring joy to everyone. Tensions ran high between Abel and Cain. No heated words. Just silence. And the silence had a chilling effect, like the coldest, deepest parts of the river shrouded in murkiness, where one could see nothing beyond the silt.

If it were possible, Calah appeared more beautiful than before, for she was deeply cherished, proving that loved women surely shine as bright as the sun, scattering their warmth to all. Edina, however, was not loved. Cain tossed her scraps of affection, just enough to keep her close to his side, but his molten gaze, more often than not, strayed to Calah and lingered as the days passed.

Eve saw covetousness in her eldest. Greed. Jealousy. How easily the names for sin came to her, especially since the taste of the Tree of Knowledge of Good and Evil still clung to her tongue, as sweet as honey and vile as sickness. She saw that sin every day, in all its forms. Adam's extreme preoccupation with work, until it bordered on obsession. Edina's hunger for acceptance, until it twisted her into another person no longer recognizable to Eve. Calah and Abel did not escape the effects of sin either. There were days when Eve despaired of ever seeing a redeemer from the fruit of her womb. No one was good enough, wise enough, kind enough to fill such a role as her Father had promised.

These thoughts plagued her as she carried a basket loaded with bounty from the orchard. She planned to view Abel's land. Abel had dug into the ground, holes placed in a circle smaller than Eve's home but large enough for a couple to enjoy. On the ground, bundles of tightly bound reeds would form the structure of the building. Abel and Adam would pull the long reeds down and secure them with ties so that they would form the roof. The reeds offered insulation from the heat, and the openings near the top of the mud-brick walls offered ventilation as the heat rose.

Eve placed the basket on the ground and rolled her shoulders to release the tension. Her tunic had stretched tight with the coming baby, and the more visible her condition, the more Adam refused to let her take part in the hard labor.

She joined her daughters beneath the shade of a rustling palm. Calah greeted her with a smile as she sat with Edina. Their nimble fingers wove a reed mat that would eventually cover the door. Abel had also planned to extend the circular design, following the pattern of a shell. It allowed him to place the door leading to the main room at a more private angle, easier to defend from predators. In the days to come, he would create a rigid screen to block the main entrance, creating two separate entrances.

It was a brilliant idea. Eve hoped Adam would do the same, especially if Cain chose to no longer sleep by the door with a spear in hand to battle whatever might creep inside.

Cain regarded the new house with his hands on his hips. For most of the morning, he had complained, barking commands, and he showed no signs of stopping. "Why don't you dig parallel holes? You could make a rectangle-shaped house instead of a circular one. The wind will blow through the windows better and you'll get a fresh breeze. It would be far larger than your current attempt."

Abel's mouth quirked as he wiped his glistening brow with the back of his hand. "Perhaps you can do that for your house. I've already dug the holes, and the design will work well enough."

A snort erupted from Cain. "The slightest puff of air will scatter your poles. With all the time you spend with your animals, it's a wonder you can even get the roof on straight."

Abel's lips thinned, but he didn't take the bait. Instead, he turned his attention to the reeds, securing the rawhide strings around the bundles.

Cain wasn't finished yet. He leaned against one of the mud-brick walls, folding his arms across his chest. "Maybe I will take your challenge. I'll make the largest house of all, with a separate shelter for the animals instead of that foul cave. I'll build something far more spacious than the hovel we live in, and I'll make it with plenty of windows so that the evening sun floods the walls with—"

"Of course you will," Calah scoffed loudly. "No one is as good as you."

Cain froze. Eve froze. Adam was nowhere in sight, having left to cut more reeds to bundle for the rest of the structure.

Without warning, Cain strode toward Calah, the dust churning beneath his bare feet. He loomed over her, his shadow long and menacing. She didn't cower, not the way Edina did, but lifted her chin in a show of defiance.

"You would do well to curb that caustic tongue of yours, Sister."

Edina blanched, her fingers stilling over the reeds. "She meant no harm, Cain. Let it go. We will build as we wish, and Abel and Calah will build as they wish, and that will be an end to it. Let them decide how to live their lives."

Eve agreed with her daughter. "I'm certain Adam would welcome your latest ideas. Why not ask him for help? Once he's finished building with Abel, of course."

"Abel always comes first, doesn't he?" Cain's voice, though soft, had enough menace to raise her hackles.

Eve was about to protest, but Cain ignored everyone but the sister he couldn't have. Bunching his massive fists, he leaned over Calah, the action menacing. "I've tolerated your insults far too long. Perhaps someone needs to put you in your place."

Calah scuttled backward, putting distance between her and her brother, her eyes widening at the threat, while Abel released the reeds at once, allowing them to snap upright with a loud swish. "Cain, that's enough!"

Eve rose to her feet, her balance slightly off with her burgeoning form. "Why not seek your father? He's feeling poorly these days, and I know he would welcome a pair of extra hands to help with the reeds."

Cain's face reddened, and he refused to tear his gaze from Calah. "I've got unfinished business right here, and I intend to be shown the proper respect."

"The proper respect?" Calah echoed loudly. She tossed her braid over her shoulder. "You are not the leader of our family. And you have done nothing to earn my respect."

Cain swung out and dug his fingers into Calah's upper arm, dragging her to her feet.

Edina squealed, Eve begged, and Abel grabbed his brother by the shoulders and pulled him back.

"Enough!" Abel spat out as he kept a white-knuckled grip on his brother's tunic. "You are not welcome here if you continue to harass my wife."

My wife.

The reminder must have stung, for Cain staggered backward, awareness seemingly flashing in his eyes. For a moment, it appeared as though he might concede. Eve sighed with relief just as Cain rushed forward, his fist colliding with Abel's jaw. The loud crack rippled through the quiet air, startling the birds in the trees. They screeched their dismay while Eve screamed, the sound unnatural in her ears.

Abel plummeted to the ground, his eyes as wide as Calah's. Rubbing his jaw, he tried to get up, but Cain pushed him a second time, forcing Abel back to the ground.

Spittle flew from Cain's mouth as he unleashed his rage while pinning Abel with his foot. "You will never lead me after Father is gone. I'll never follow you, do you hear me? I don't care whose favor you steal, whether it's God's or our parents'.

You've twisted how everyone perceives me because of your lies. If you hadn't given an animal sacrifice, I know God would have approved of mine."

Abel brushed aside his brother and leaped to his feet.

Before anyone else could get hurt, Eve pushed herself between the brothers, a hard enough task with her protruding belly. She planted both palms on Cain's chest, but it was like pressing against the cave wall. Her eldest refused to budge, choosing instead to advance. She stumbled but kept her hands on his chest.

Her protest was just as feeble a barrier as her hands. "No, Cain. No one has poisoned us against you. Abel has not lied about you. And no one can deceive God. He sees through each of us. He sees us for who we truly are."

"Get. Out. Of. My. Way," Cain enunciated, baring his white teeth at Eve. Before she could answer, he reached out with his long arm, as big as Adam's, and swept her easily away like a leaf floating on the river.

But she had delayed her eldest long enough for Abel to regain his balance. He took her place, refusing to move. Both men collided once again, one grunting and furious, and the other calm. Abel wrapped his fingers into a fistful of Cain's tunic once again and jerked his brother forward.

"For too long, you've tracked Calah's footsteps. No more will you wait for her in the orchards, nor follow her to the fields, nor watch her near the meadows. I won't tolerate it." Abel released his fistful of Cain's tunic as if he had touched something distasteful. "Leave my home now."

"You can't make me do anything," Cain taunted as he straightened his stained tunic.

Abel remained resolute as he stared into his brother's eyes. "Out of respect for our parents, I won't hurt you. But don't test me again."

Despite the quivering in her limbs, Eve spoke, keeping her voice soothing and intentionally soft. "Go get some rest, Cain. Eat something. We'll talk later."

Cain flicked a hard glance at her and strode away without another word or apology. Edina remained alone on the mat, her expression stricken.

"He'll feel better after he's had a day or two alone," Eve confided to her other children. But Abel's look of disbelief sent shame slithering through her. Would Cain truly feel peace with nothing more than a nap and a hearty meal?

Calah stood to her feet and brushed her tunic free of dirt and a few brown leaves clinging to the soft leather. "Mama, he needs to do more than simply leave my home. He must leave our entire homestead and never return. Don't you see how destructive he's turning? Abel is right. Cain hasn't left me alone. Worse, he's cruel to Edina."

"No, no!" Edina pushed up from the ground, her eyes welling with tears. "Tell them not to turn on him, Mama. He needs us. He just needs some more tenderness. We can save him if we refuse to give up on him."

Those had been Eve's very words for years. She had believed them. Still believed them, but Cain...Cain tested every boundary she had, including those of the others.

"I can't take any more fighting. The only time we have peace is when he disappears for days on end without warning." Calah's voice rose louder. "He has no right to live next to us and make us endure his misery!"

"Shh," Eve hushed her daughter more sharply than she intended. "I don't want him hearing what you said. Why must you stir trouble further?"

"You've protected him more than any of us, Mama! How could you? How can you be so blind to what is in front of you?" Calah rushed away, sobbing as she fled in the riverbank's direction.

Edina turned her back to Eve. She snatched one of the empty baskets. "You are all so judgmental. So quick to blame Cain for everything." With that, Edina marched in the opposite direction. "You are wrong about him, and one day, you'll regret how you've hurt him."

Eve held her hand to her mouth, quelling the rising cry within her.

What a mess, Father. I can do nothing right. I cannot even raise my children to love each other.

A thick arm wrapped around her shoulder and pulled her close. She smelled Abel, the musky scent of animals and sweat and dried reeds mingling on his leather tunic. He said nothing as he held her close.

"Oh Mama," he rasped as his green eyes blazed with concern, "you are crying."

She nodded.

He raised her chin with his calloused hands. It was like peering into a younger, tender version of Adam. "I'm so sorry we've hurt you. You must remember that we love you. Each of your children."

She hiccupped, her throat sore from weeping. "But I've failed each of you. It breaks my heart to see such fighting, such division among us. If only I could fix everything as simply as plastering mud and filling the cracks in the wall. I would do whatever it takes."

"You've tried. But we each have our own will. We each make our choices. You know, I've long considered, had I been the one who stood in front of the Tree of Knowledge of Good and Evil, what would I have done? I've asked God to show me the truth. I believe, Mama, and I don't say this lightly, that I too would have rebelled and eaten from it. Perhaps I would have made a far worse representation of man than either you or Father. Who's saying I wouldn't have been glutted with pride and power? I wrestle enough with them as it is."

She tapped him on the shoulder. "Don't you say such things. God promised me a redeemer who would come from my seed. One who would destroy the lies of the serpent and make everything right again."

Abel watched her as she dried her tears with the back of her hand. She continued, her hopes and dreams resting on the one who stood before her. "At first, I thought the redeemer might be Cain. Then I hoped he would be you."

Abel stepped backward, releasing his hold on her. "I cannot fathom God's will in this, but one way or another, I believe He will fulfill His promise in His way. Together, you and I will trust Him, won't we? He is a good and gracious God, full of mercy. We must trust Him."

It was both strange and wonderful hearing her own advice served back to her. She cupped Abel's cheek. "I am so proud of you, my son. How much joy you've brought me! I love you more than life itself. God gave me one of the greatest gifts when I first held you as a newborn. Now look at the man you've become. How blessed you are, touched with God's favor."

He ducked his head as if embarrassed by her lavish praise. "I had the best of mothers."

Before she could protest and exclaim that she was the *only* mother, he soundly kissed her cheek and returned to his work on the house.

CHAPTER TWENTY-FOUR

Cain did not return to Eve's home during the night. She had waited for him despite Adam's whispered protests to return to bed. Calah and Abel stayed in their tent, next to the circular house that would soon belong to them. Edina curled next to the door, waiting for Cain. Eve sat with her beloved daughter's head on her lap. They waited throughout much of the night, as Eve brushed Edina's hair, whispering love and encouragement. Praying her daughter would stay close to her.

The quiet hush at dawn felt almost unbearable when she dwelt on the previous fight. Dare Eve ask Cain to leave the entire homestead?

Adam had no advice either, when she asked his opinion. Instead, he palmed the back of his neck, his face drawn in weary lines.

He was far too worried about repairing the rock wall and ensuring the meadow remained safe from predators. Yet even Adam had been moved from his granite expression when she detailed the violence of the fight.

"I'll find Cain and speak with him," her husband promised with a long-suffering sigh.

But would he fulfill that promise, or would he leave her to deal with Cain alone? She dreaded the encounter, weighing every option. Asking Cain to leave felt far too harsh a punishment. Asking him to stay would ensure far more fighting, as the past had proven.

What to do?

Eve distracted herself with the easiest of chores until a series of contractions forced her to drop her basket and clutch the rock wall lining the fields for support. She closed her eyes and inhaled deeply to slow the rapid pulse threatening to take flight. She had Edina and Calah. She would be fine.

Yet neither could she discount the fact that this pregnancy felt different from the others. More insistent, somehow. Yesterday and into this morning, the baby had remained strangely motionless, as if preparing for the big moment.

"Patience, darling one," she whispered through the contraction. "It's too soon for you to arrive."

To her relief, the baby wiggled, as if to disagree.

Chuckling, Eve reached for her basket. She saw no sign of Calah in the orchard. Perhaps her daughter had other tasks to attend to this early morning. Amid the solitude of the fruit trees, surrounded by the sound of rustling leaves and dangling peaches, Eve picked what she could, welcoming the reprieve of silence.

When she returned home, Adam smeared fresh mud along the wall, repairing sections of the crumbling stones. He waved at her, his face relaxed despite the tension of the previous day. Edina and Calah hadn't returned for the afternoon meal. Instead, as Edina had noted the previous day, they would finish weaving the mat to cover the door and help Abel secure the reeds. Abel planned to stake out a fence for his new field later in the day while Edina and Calah finished the final touches to the house, including plastering the walls with mud.

No one knew what Cain planned to do next. Perhaps he would simply take another one of his unannounced excursions and leave without a word for days on end.

Eve was about to deposit her basket inside the house when a guttural scream shattered the sound of birds chirping. It happened a second time, echoing across the meadow. Eve dropped her basket, the peaches rolling on the grass. She ran despite the babe in her womb. Adam joined her as well, abandoning his wall.

In the distance, a figure ran, arms waving wildly and hair streaming. It was Calah, pumping her legs as fast as she could, eating up the distance of the meadow.

Calah threw her arms around Adam, weeping so hard she couldn't speak. Adam wrapped his daughter in a fierce hug. She pulled back, her eyes shining with tears. "Father, come quickly. I found Abel in our field."

Nothing could prepare Eve for what she would see next. She had witnessed the majestic beauty of Eden and the unfathomable creativity of her Father. She had witnessed the terrifying power of the cherubim. She had faced the wicked serpent and eaten from the forbidden tree.

She thought she had seen the full extent of evil until now. When the three of them reached the newly outlined field, the ground freshly charred from a recent fire to prepare the land, Abel lay face down in the ash and dirt, his body contorted at an odd angle.

But worse than the strange crook of his neck was the pool of blood now matted in the long locks of his hair and sliding down into his tunic, staining it a deep brownish red.

She flung herself beside her boy, running her hands against his shoulders, his arms—already so cold, so hard to the touch, as if he had been turned to stone.

"He is dead," Adam said in shock. "Our son is dead." And then he pivoted and threw up, heaving his breakfast of mangoes and avocados all over his tunic and bare feet.

"No, no," Eve murmured over and over as she felt for some telltale sign of a beating heart or the faint quiver of a pulse along Abel's wrists. But he did not answer to Calah's sobs, or Adam's groans, nor to her motherly demands that he awaken.

Abel was gone. Forever from this world.

Separated from God, and now her child?

Dimly she heard Adam's furious questions, hurled as rapidly as spears. "Where is Cain? Where is Edina? Why are they not here?"

"I don't know, Father," Calah rasped as her unfocused gaze darted wildly between Eve and Adam. "Cain told Abel to meet him in the field at dawn. They argued again last night over the sacrifices. Cain continued to accuse Abel of turning God against him. I know Abel hoped to find peace with Cain this morning. If I had known this would happen, I would never have let Abel meet with him."

Adam sank to his knees as if overwhelmed. His jaw hung slack. "Why? Why would our eldest do such a thing? Why would he kill his younger brother?"

Calah shuddered visibly as she wrapped her arms tight over her middle. "Cain hates Abel."

Abel's matted hair, his long lashes closed as if in sleep, brought bile rising within her. Eve pressed a fist against her mouth. Surely this was nothing more than a nightmare. Surely she would awaken and find her family as they once were.

"Cain is nowhere to be found?" Adam demanded sharply.

Calah shook her head.

No one could hide better in the woods than Cain. No one had dared leave as much as he had.

"And of course, Edina followed." Eve laid her head against Abel's strong shoulder, seeking what comfort she could find. She wanted to weep, but she couldn't. It was as if a numb, deep void yawned inside of her, threatening to devour her whole.

Calah twisted her hands together, her expression grief-stricken. "Yes, she will never leave him. He's made her such promises, and she can't seem to free herself. None of us would be able convince her otherwise."

"Oh God, why?" Adam suddenly howled as he clawed at his tunic as if to shred it. Ashes fluttered near Abel, and Adam picked up a handful, smearing himself with the dirt and ash, dragging the filth across his chest. "Why have You allowed this to happen to us, to our sons?"

Anger filled Eve, mingled with disbelief. She balled her fists as she stared at Adam. "You promised me you would talk with Cain this morning. Why didn't you, when you had the chance? Perhaps the questions lie with us, Adam. Why didn't you show more love to your eldest when he needed it so?"

Adam staggered back as if an asp had struck him. "Me? Why did you coddle him for years on end, caving in to his every demand, making excuses for his bad choices? If you hadn't tempted me with that fruit—"

She leaped to her feet, her voice strangely not her own. White-hot fury ripped through her, burning away any last restraint. "If you had stopped me from eating it, none of this would have happened! Adam, you watched me. You watched me be deceived, and not once did you try to yank the fruit from my hand or slap my arm so that I would drop it. You stood there and did *nothing*."

He rose to his full height. And before she knew it, they were hurling accusations and insults, recalling every single wrong, every broken promise, every failure that either of them had committed since they had left the garden.

"Stop!" Calah cried. "Oh, stop! Please, I beg you. Abel wouldn't want us to fight over him like this. Please, Father. Please, Mama. Cain did this wicked thing. He is entirely to blame for his choices, as we all are. Oh, please don't degrade Abel's memory by attacking each other."

Eve heaved, her lungs struggling to take in a breath. Her ears rang and her heart felt as though it might explode. Near the copse a rattle came from the cypress trees. A sickening rattle—one that reminded of Eden and the white serpent. A sickly-sweet voice, one she recognized, whispered in her ear.

"You are all alone, little one. Your God has abandoned you, hasn't He? You are of no further use to Him. It would be better for you to give in and fade away."

The serpent spoke her greatest fear. To be so forgotten, so unwanted, and so lost, that God would never choose to find her. She tried to open her mouth and speak, but the chill had extended to each of her limbs, paralyzing her.

"Oh God, please help us," she finally cried out loud. "We need You."

As quickly as the serpent appeared, he left at her plea for help, but she felt his presence. And the stench of death and decay lingered on the breeze.

Adam and Calah didn't appear to see or hear the serpent. Instead, they gaped at her as if she had turned into a madwoman, Calah's jaw working as she tried to contain her grief, and Adam...Adam looked as though he too might die.

She had said things she couldn't take back. Horrible things in a moment of extreme passion, each barb strong enough to destroy whatever remained of her relationship with Adam. And Adam, too, had shredded her to pieces with his savage accusations.

Another pain stabbed her belly, and she doubled over, moaning as a new life demanded entrance into this broken, hurting world.

"I'm going to bury our son. Alone." Adam said as his gaze slid to Eve's. So much anguish lived in those green eyes. "Take your mother home, Calah."

The labor occurred all too quickly, especially after Eve's water broke. By the time she reached the comfort of her home, Calah thankfully took charge. She lowered Eve onto the mat, murmuring encouragement, though she had never witnessed a complete birth considering Eve's previous miscarriages.

"I should get Father." Calah knelt beside Eve, sliding a leather pillow stuffed with grass beneath Eve's head. One lovingly stitched by Edina.

"No time," Eve gasped. Bittersweet memories filled her as she strained, the pain, for once, a welcome relief to the numbness inside her soul.

Why are You giving me another child, Father? I'm unworthy.

She heard no audible voice answer her, but her spirit rebelled as soon as the thought crossed her mind. Was the serpent lying to her at this moment?

Another memory rode over the falsehoods demanding obedience.

You are My beloved daughter.

She grabbed fistfuls of the wraps by her side and pushed with all her might.

"And I will put enmity between you and the woman, and between your offspring and hers; he will crush your head and you will strike his heel."

God had promised her deliverance. *He promised.*

But now, whatever she had tried to build, to keep, to protect, lay ruined beyond her imagination.

Again, the thought wouldn't quite let her go. *You are My beloved daughter, Eve.*

Exhausted, she could do nothing more than rest against the pillow while a cry resounded in the room.

"You have a daughter, Mama! She is exquisite," Calah exclaimed as she helped prepare the newborn, snatching a spare tunic to wrap the baby in the folds. "What will you name her?"

A baby girl, with a lusty cry, nestled onto Eve's chest to nurse. She looked nothing like Calah or Edina. "Ariel." Lioness of God.

"A worthy name," Calah whispered with tears in her eyes as she watched Ariel nurse. While Eve rested, Calah found other things to do, as if she feared rest.

Eve held her newborn close while the sounds of noisy sucking filled the room. Adam had yet to return. He was right. He would have another daughter. But there would be no rejoicing or laughter tonight.

Instead, there would only be grief.

CHAPTER TWENTY-FIVE

In the days that followed, Calah moved back into Eve's home. She lavished love on Ariel but kept distant from Eve. Adam remained remote as well, choosing to reside in the tent that once was Abel's. He came home to hold Ariel and kiss Calah on the head. But for Eve, there was only silence.

The wounds were so deep, she feared neither of them would heal.

When Eve was strong enough to walk, she made her way to the river where Cain had likely traversed. She traveled as far as she dared, knowing she would need to return soon to nurse Ariel. Her youngest gave her the will to survive, but not much more. Eve felt more like a husk than a woman, more dust than living.

And although she had reached the point along the river where the waters dipped to shallow depths, she realized she could go no farther.

There would be no following her sons or daughter. She would never see Abel again in this world, and if Cain wandered where his heart desired, she would likely never see him again, or Edina. What would they encounter out in the wild? Would he finally learn to be kind to Edina and their children? What would happen to Calah now that no sons remained for her to marry? Would her daughter remain alone until it was too late?

How could Eve possibly forgive Cain for what he had done, his actions destroying her family?

Some thoughts were far too painful to contemplate as Eve paused by the river to wash her face and burning eyes.

She had lost three adult children. One remained estranged, though respectful. Her husband had left her. It was punishment enough to contemplate her mistakes, but fear for her children and the paths they might take—it was more than a woman could bear alone.

Beside her, the swirling currents of the river leading out of Eden continued as if nothing had changed. But everything had changed.

Adam's cry was her own. She yelled into the breeze, her arms outstretched. "Why, God? Why, Father, have You allowed so much pain? Why even let us live if this is all that is left?"

The wind brushed her cheeks as tenderly as a caress, but her Father was not in the wind. Nor in the bright blue sky above, nor in the trees swaying with each gust.

Yet somehow, she sensed He was near. Near enough to hear her cry. The omniscient, the omnipresent, the omnipotent, as Adam had once described Him when they had pointed to the stars in the sky on their beloved hill. The all-knowing, ever-present and all-powerful God who had spoken the universe into existence. The One who would make everything right again.

The love she had felt when she first awakened suffused her, supernatural and far more powerful than the serpent's curses. She reached out her hand to touch the sky and, if possible, let Him know that she still sought Him.

"Oh Father, I have nothing left to give. And I am so very lost."

But He had promised deliverance. His word remained true. And she would keep clinging to that promise until her life faded from her. Who was she to fight against her Father's sovereign will? For some reason, He had allowed this suffering to occur.

Hadn't she told Cain that God disciplined those He loved? That sin brought a cost?

She had blamed Adam for so long for so many things. And she was tired of blaming others. She was tired of trying to be perfect enough to regain entrance into Eden.

Falling to her knees, she bowed her head. "I need You, Father. Forgive me for sinning against You in Eden. Adam was right. Forgive me for the mistakes I've made with my children. Forgive me for all the anger and rage within my soul. Forgive my spirit of discontent. I've accused Adam of weakness when I've had the same weakness within me. I'm surrendering everything. Myself. I'm surrendering my children to You. I can't fix what they've done, or what I've done. None of us can ever reach Your righteousness without Your help. I've tried so hard to be good enough, but I can't bridge the gap between You and me. Please have mercy on us. Have mercy on me. If possible, heal what remains of my family. I can't do this with only my strength."

Her confession felt good and right, but something was missing. At once, she saw Adam's haggard features and all the ways he had tried as hard as she had to be good and just, albeit differently. Had he tried to chase away his immense grief with work? And now he too had lost nearly everything. She had asked for compassion for herself and for Cain, but what about Adam?

Mercy for her husband replaced the old resentment. "Help Adam. He must feel so lost right now. Help him know that he is truly not alone. That he is beloved. Help me show him love."

No, they could not earn their way back to Eden. But God would make a way. She sensed His love, His forgiveness, His assurance.

Leaves swirled around her, and the grass bowed with her as the wind picked up speed and rushed toward Cain's plateau. The supernatural peace, one that she had not felt since Eden, grew and grew in her heart, like the roots of a tree digging deep into her soul. As she rose to her feet, she felt her Father's assurance.

Her children were no longer her sole burden to carry. Her Father would watch over them. He would arrange their steps if they sought Him.

It was not too late for her or her family. Not all was lost. She could only trust in His promises and be patient with His timing. Grief would come again and trials too. But as she made her way back home, she sensed He would never leave her.

And she would never stop seeking Him.

After returning home, her heart lighter following her time alone with God, Eve nursed Ariel and laid her baby down on a nest of blankets for a nap.

"I'm going to find your father," Eve told Calah, who was roasting vegetables on a spit over the open fire. "He cannot continue to grieve alone. If I can, I will bring him back."

Calah nodded, her features pensive as she looked over her shoulder. Twilight would soon bathe the land in shades of purple. "I'll send you with food. Don't worry about Ariel. I'll watch over her like she was my own."

Eve carefully wrapped the vegetables and a mango in a frond. Her heart pounded as she followed the worn path leading toward Abel's field. The ground remained scorched, a testament to the destruction. In the center of the field, her husband sat, his shoulders hunched. He hadn't dipped into the river, nor changed his tunic. Instead, he sat with his arms clasped about his legs and his head on his knees.

The faint sound of sobbing reached her ears. She paused midstep, afraid to go to him. Oh, the things she had said! If only she could take back her reckless anger.

Go. Go to him.

She felt the words as clearly as if they had been spoken. With a silent pleading for help, she tiptoed, her bare feet making no sound in the powdery dirt. As quietly as she could, she set the satchel next to him. Then she cleared her throat. "Adam, I realize you may not want me here. But I ask your forgiveness for so many things. For offering you the fruit of the Tree of Knowledge of Good and Evil. For not listening to your concerns about our children, especially Cain. For all those awful fights when we were younger."

Her voice broke as she reached out to finger his hair and touch his cheek while he remained sitting. "If I could take away everything and return us to the garden and our wonderful hill, I would. I miss you. I've always missed you since we fled Eden. But I want you to know how much I love you and will always love you."

His shoulders heaved once, then nothing.

When she stepped backward to return home, he turned in one swift motion and wrapped his arms around her waist and wept, his head pressed into the worn folds of her tunic. She let him weep, her hands smoothing his hair as she whispered of love and shared grief.

He tugged on her hand until she sat down, and to her surprise, he pulled her onto his lap and rested his forehead against hers. "Eve, I will always love you. I was so afraid you would never want me again as your husband."

"No, I was afraid you might leave forever," she whispered, leaning against his damp tunic.

He shook his head, his voice thick with emotion. "I will never leave you. I've spent the last few days and nights wrestling with all that's happened. You were not wrong about challenging me. I was too proud to admit I was wrong about so many things. I should have stopped you from eating the fruit. I knew what would happen. The serpent did not deceive me. Stopping you would have been the loving thing to do. But I was weak, and I didn't want to face the depths of my mistakes all these years. In the end, I pushed you and Cain—pushed all of us to be better, to overcome our failings. These past days,

I've had to come face-to-face with my sin. I must beg your forgiveness. I wish I had shown more grace, more compassion to you and Cain. When I should have spoken with him over the fight, I lost my courage and kept silent. I failed my son, and I failed you."

"And I wish I had been stronger to discipline him," she whispered, her throat raw. "So it appears we both were right and wrong regarding how to raise our family."

His arms tightened around her, pulling her snug against his beating chest. But his next admission sent a tremor rippling down her spine. "I felt moved to speak to Father on your behalf, to ask Him to protect you this morning. I don't know what you saw after Abel died, something in the forest, but I felt an evil presence. It was so overpowering, all I wanted was to lie down and sleep and never awaken. But I begged God to help, and He brought me peace. I was about to go find you when I saw you come over the hill, like an answer to my prayer."

Had Adam talked to God at the same moment she had? Hope unfurled within her, like the fragile growth in a field.

He whispered into her ear, earning another shiver. "I've asked God to forgive me for my sin and selfishness. Will you, Eve, forgive me? I am unworthy to be your husband, but with our Father's help, I will do better."

How long they sat together, with arms entwined, hearts nearly beating as one, she did not know. They spoke of many things, and she could not deny her reluctance to return home. When had she had time just alone with him to sit and talk together as they had in the early days?

He talked about Abel, mentioning his son's dreams and plans, the silly quirks of how Abel liked to tease his sisters and how well he took care of the flock, and then...hesitantly about Cain.

"Will you seek Cain and Edina?" she asked, still snug in her husband's arms.

"No," Adam answered slowly. "I want to find them. More than anything, I want to tell Cain and Edina that I love them, but I feel I must wait. When God moves and tells me otherwise, I will obey."

A sigh escaped her at the idea of her two lost children so alone in the world, with no one to guide them, especially God.

"I know," Adam murmured in sympathy as he hugged her again. "I know. God isn't finished with them yet. They are in His hands, not ours."

"I agree." She raised her head and studied the sky with Adam by her side. Above them, the sun peeked through the clouds while hawks soared overhead. "If our Father can create all of this, then surely He can watch over our children."

Adam smiled at her—a small smile, but a smile nonetheless.

She had feared tragedy would split the two of them in half, forcing them to different paths. Instead, a shifting in the relationship occurred. A new tenderness. A healing. She welcomed it, deciding right then and there she would never again fling the past in his face, or his old failures. Together, they would work hard to build a life together, one of respect and kindness. One in which they would truly listen to each other.

With his arm still about her waist, he brushed his lips against her cheek. "Come, Eve, let's go home."

CHAPTER TWENTY-SIX

Grief took many stages for Eve and her family, which, though smaller, felt somehow stronger than ever before. She and Calah still wept when one of them encountered something of Abel's. Calah wore the shell necklace each day, her fingers straying to stroke the frayed leather strand. The days moved slowly, relief found with Ariel's sweet gurgles and dimpled smiles.

One morning, when stumbling across a rotten egg, Calah raised her hand and covered her mouth, her eyes watering.

Eve could only stare at her daughter as comprehension dawned. "You're pregnant."

A light lit Calah's eyes as she wiped her foot on the grass and moved away from the offensive egg. "I had wondered when Abel was alive, but it was too soon to tell. Now, I know for certain."

Adam rejoiced with Calah, and he made plans to finish the house that Abel had started so that Calah could have a place of her own if she so desired. She readily agreed. To Eve's surprise, the slight distance benefited their relationship, and she grew closer to Calah as the seasons changed and the birds migrated farther south.

One afternoon, when Eve and Calah spread a fresh coat of mud over the interior walls of Abel's home, Calah paused before she looked Eve in the eye.

"There were moments when I almost hated you," she admitted. "But now that I have my child coming soon, I think I understand why you loved Cain so deeply, Mama. I understand why you couldn't let him go."

"I made so many mistakes," Eve readily admitted. "It's a wonder that you and Abel believed in God. Yet despite my mistakes, I believe my Father drew you and Abel. That gives me hope for Ariel and for Cain and for Edina. He has forgiven me. He will forgive those who seek Him. I will no longer see your father's sacrifices as a useless thing. Hope remains, because God forgives us."

"Sometimes I fear it is far harder to forgive oneself," Calah mused as she dipped her hand into the leather bucket and withdrew more mud. "I have lain awake many nights wondering how things would be different if only I hadn't goaded Cain when I did. Abel certainly paid the price."

"No, Cain made his choices, Calah. He was fighting against God at every step and resented your brother's obedience. Don't blame yourself for Cain's jealousy over the one God chose to favor. A reasonable man wouldn't have killed a brother over a sacrifice. Do not take that burden," Eve said firmly as she covered the cracks in the wall.

Calah touched the shells draped around her neck. "I've longed for this child. It will be as if we have a part of Abel remaining with us."

Eve's throat tightened as she glanced at Ariel, who watched them with wide eyes from her place of comfort on the floor. "I've so wanted you to have a helpmate again, to know the joy I've found with your father."

Calah's eyes watered as she scooped up more mud with her fingers and smeared it across the wall. "I'm content with my life, Mama. It isn't what I hoped for, but I believe that God will make something beautiful out of what was broken. I'm grateful for what I have. I have you and Father and Ariel. And now this child. Our homestead will be filled with the sounds of life and joy again."

Eve treasured her daughter's words, storing them deep within for the moments when grief threaten to overtake her. Calah was right. Joy came, slowly but surely, as the seasons changed and the birds returned to nest in the trees. Recent growth poked through the blackened fields, including Abel's. In the months that followed, Calah delivered a healthy boy. She named him Alon, like the sapling oak tree that had sprouted next to her home, promising shelter.

Eve celebrated with her daughter, while Ariel, who was but a baby yet sucking on her thumb, followed the newborn's movements with her wide eyes. Somehow, Eve felt those two would be the best of friends, just as Abel and Calah had been.

Day by day, she released her expectations of what life should be. She released the desire for control, and whenever she felt the urge to find out what was happening to Cain, she knelt down on her mat and beseeched her Father to intervene.

She bathed Cain and Edina in tear-soaked prayers. But not one word came regarding her lost children.

And then, many years later, when Alon and Ariel had married and had grandchildren and great-grandchildren of their own, Adam brought news after an extended hunting trip. "I found our son and daughter. Cain and Edina have had many children and grandchildren. He settled near the river farther south and built a large house. It would take at least nine days to get there. While following a herd of deer, I stumbled across their homestead. I didn't speak to anyone. From a distance, I observed them."

"We all should greet them," she exclaimed, her mama's heart yearning to see her children and grandchildren.

"I will visit first," Adam reached out and caressed her cheek. "Let me see if Cain has truly changed."

In the old days, she would have argued, but now, she listened to her husband's concern. Adam kissed her before traveling with Alon.

After fifteen days, fifteen long days, she spied her husband and grandson emerging from the forest surrounding her house. Weariness marked each of Adam's movements. When she ran to greet him, he could barely smile.

She brushed his cheek with her fingertips. "You look sad."

A rare quaver entered his voice, making him appear vulnerable. "I fear Cain has not changed. Instead, he has hardened. As has Edina. They don't worship God the way we do. Cain has embellished our stories and perverted them into things I don't recognize. He built a room onto his house dedicated to worship, but I saw the image of the snake carved into the clay pillars. There are so many family members. Children upon children, and each one of them is lost. I tried to tell them of Eden, and of Father, and the Tree of Knowledge of Good and Evil. Cain told me to leave and never return."

So, the serpent had not vanished after all. Instead, he had found new ways to deceive.

"Did he say anything about Abel?" Dare she hope her eldest showed some remorse for his actions?

Adam reached for her hand. In that moment, he appeared old to her. His black hair gleamed with far more white, as if somehow, he had aged overnight. "I heard some of the story. God spoke to Cain and asked him where Abel was."

God had intervened?

She pressed her hand against her chest, the old ache flaring up again.

Adam continued, "And predictably, our son said, 'Am I my brother's keeper?'"

"No!" she protested, horrified at such a careless response. So cold and so dishonest.

The light in Adam's eyes died. He ducked his head as if ashamed on behalf of his son. "You and I both know God cannot be deceived. He challenged our son. 'What have you done? The voice of your brother's blood is crying to me from the ground. And now you are cursed from the ground, which has opened its mouth to receive your brother's blood from your hand. When you work the ground, it shall no longer yield to you its strength. You shall be a fugitive and a wanderer on the earth.'"

"But he is not a wanderer. He has built this city, as you witnessed."

Her husband paused, his throat bobbing with effort. "Trust Cain to do as he pleases. He dared to argue with God, but said,

'My punishment is greater than I can bear. Behold, you have driven me today away from the ground, and from your face I shall be hidden. I shall be a fugitive and a wanderer on earth. Whoever finds me will kill me."

She gasped. "But we would never hurt our child. Never!"

"God put a mark on him. If anyone kills Cain, vengeance shall be taken on him sevenfold."

Such news brought no closure or comfort. Only more questions. *Why?* Why had Cain allowed so much jealousy over Abel's worship to drive such rebellion? Why had Cain rejected God over and over? God had not been unfair. He had not placed undue burdens on any of them.

"Did he ask about me or Calah?"

"No, not really." Adam unslung his bag and let it drop to the ground. "He only wants to talk about his city, named after his son Enoch. They wish to keep expanding and eventually fill the entire plain with their grandeur. I understand some of our great-great grandchildren have mastered the art of melting metals. Some of them play music on stringed instruments. I've never seen such ingenuity or such artistry."

"Enoch," she whispered, tasting the name. Her grandson. She might never be free to share her story with him.

Adam reached for her hand and raised it to his mouth, pressing a kiss against her knuckles. "I know hearing this hurts, Eve, but Cain asked us not to return. I think he feels shame or fear regarding his deeds. But I do have peace regarding our children. Edina wanted me to send you a gift. She made a leather bag for you. She misses you terribly."

Eve closed her eyes briefly. The image of her daughter as a child, sitting by the fire with a needle and thread in her hand brought a fearsome ache.

"I wish I could send her a gift. Does he treat her well?"

But Adam didn't know. He had tried to speak with Edina privately and found he couldn't, thanks to Cain's insistence. Again, Eve had more questions than answers.

"It seems I must trust God a while longer," she said as she took the bag Adam handed her. Tracing her fingers across the tooled leather brought swift longing and another plea that her Father would watch over His children.

In the seasons that followed, Eve watched her family grow until fields stretched out in every direction and houses rose around hers. The laughter of children filled the orchard, along with sounds of building. Calah found a gray hair or two, just like Eve. Life continued, a slow march marked by the constellations.

Eve continued as she always had, planting her herbal garden, stocking her medicinal supplies and teaching her offspring. But always, running through the back of her mind, like the endless wind whispering through the trees, were thoughts of those she had lost.

The pain had lessened, but the memories remained as sharp and as vivid as ever. Grief had a way of dimming her smile or stealing her attention from those in front of her.

One morning, when Alon and Ariel were tending the fields with Calah, there was no one else but Eve at home—a rare respite from her brood. The curtain brushed aside, and Adam entered just as she sat down in front of the loom trailing with dyed wool.

"A lamb wandered away, and I need your help to retrieve her."

She didn't need to be asked twice to leave the house. Grabbing her satchel of medicinal supplies and wrappings, she followed him into the meadow where the birds trilled.

Adam glanced at her. "I heard bleating past the cave. When I climbed the rocks, I found the lamb trapped between the rocky ledges, jammed into a narrow space of a ravine. I can descend, but I'll need a hand to help me climb back up again. Especially if I hold her with one arm."

Adam's knees weren't as limber as they once were, even if his shoulders remained broad and muscled.

She slung her satchel over her shoulder. "Poor thing. I've brought what I can to help."

Without warning, Adam reached for her hand, entwining his fingers with hers, swinging her arm back and forth like the earliest of days. With sun on her head and back, and her husband's smile, it was the closest thing she could remember to Eden.

His dimples creased on either side as he flashed her a white grin. And before she knew it, he no longer held her hand, because his arm had wrapped about her waist.

As they approached the cave and the enormous rocky ledge jutting outward, he held out his hand to help her climb alongside him. Beyond the cave, where the rocks pushed together as if squished like lumps of clay, a bleating intensified.

"We're here. Be patient, Reena." Adam cupped his hand over his mouth.

"Reena?"

He winked at her. "You know I name my favorite sheep."

The bleating paused. And just as Adam had promised, in the narrowest of ledges leading toward a ravine, a lamb was wedged on the smallest of outcroppings. Somehow it had stumbled into peril while running away from the flock.

With a low groan, Adam peered over the edge. "What I need is a stick. With a hook on the end of it."

She laughed to think of such an image of Adam hooking a lamb. But all jests aside, he would find a way to make one, chiseling the wood with his beloved obsidian blades.

Finding cracks in the rock face, he carefully stretched himself and descended, toehold by toehold and fingerhold by fingerhold, inching toward the lost lamb. He slipped once and swung himself back onto the nearest ledge before reaching with one long arm and snagging the lamb with a tight grip.

Eve managed to swallow a gasp and lay flat on the rock, holding out her hand so he could hoist himself up easier. His green eyes sought her, all humor fleeing when he tried to find another outcropping to climb to her. With the wiggling lamb pinned beneath one arm, he reached out for her.

She clung with all her might, her fingers straining beneath his weight. He slipped, a groan escaping him when he failed to brace himself with his toes. She reached down with her other arm and pulled again, his bulk dragging her toward the treacherous edge as pebbles dug into her skin.

But she would not let go.

"Almost there," she encouraged breathlessly as she tugged him with all her might. When he found a new crack in the rocks with his feet, he surged forward, pushing the lamb into her arms and latching onto the ledge with both hands.

One heave, and he was beside her while she tightly held the trembling lamb.

No broken bones. No deep gouges. The lamb seemed to know it was safe in her arms.

When she raised her head, her gaze collided with her husband's. Bright green. Intense.

"What would I do without you, Eve?" he murmured, his eyes suspiciously moist.

She chuckled and then sobered when he reached out to cup her cheek. "Or I, you. I'm not going anywhere soon, Adam."

The lamb lay forgotten beside her when he pulled her to him. One arm encircled her waist and the other entangled in her hair. He kissed her deeply. All thoughts fled her mind except for him.

His endearments and praise were all the more precious to her these days. Adam had changed. He was softer. Kinder. Quicker to listen when needed, more apt to speak when the circumstance dictated. As the seasons passed and age crept in, Eve thought her beloved, despite the wrinkles lining his brow, more beautiful and wise than the perfect Adam she once knew.

With a sigh, he rested his head against hers. "Not a day goes by when I don't thank God for you. I could not ask for a better partner."

Despite the brokenness, the trials, the grief, and the disappointment, they had emerged stronger together, fused in purpose and finally working together as one.

And if love was like this...full of mercy and sacrifice and endurance, then she felt as if she had been given a taste of Eden again.

When Eve and Adam entered the homestead, the entire family gathered as one and cried out, waving their arms in welcome to see the first Mother and Father return with the lost lamb.

A meal waited by the firepit, the roasted vegetables and grains mixed with fragrant herbs. The smallest of the children followed Adam as he placed the lost lamb back in the pen. After he washed his hands and face, he returned to the crackling fire.

"I sometimes think these lost lambs are just like me," Adam told everyone over the flames. "And God, in His mercy, finds us and redeems us."

When his gaze met hers, his features illuminated with the orange glow, she saw peace again. Understanding, silent but aware, passed between them.

"Perhaps the lamb strays for a long time and finds itself in a dangerous ravine, surrounded by predators. But no situation is too difficult for our Father. He alone can save us. Even from ourselves."

She sucked in a breath, rejoicing to hear Adam speak more and more of God to his family. He asked each family member to join him around the fire every evening. Discussing God became a thing to be cherished, not endured with clenched teeth. The children threw questions at Adam, and he answered each one as patiently as he could. At long last, both Adam and Even fully shared the responsibility of raising the next generation.

The image of the lost lamb stayed with her for many seasons. If God could care for that lamb, surely this was proof He would look after her family. He would watch over Cain and Edina, come what may. Her son's actions still hurt her, but she could breathe again. She could live her life and continue to discover God's purpose for her life.

Her Father, however, was not finished with her.

On Adam's one hundred and thirtieth birthday, when his body remained as strong and virile as ever but most of his hair glinted with threads of moonlight, she told him they would have another baby.

On the day of his birth, she crooned over her newborn son, rocking him just as she had with her other children. The baby blinked at her with brilliant blue eyes, sure to change color one day. But the pain of the past, though it would never disappear, was replaced with gratitude. Adam named the boy Seth.

"God has brought an anointing, a compensation." Adam explained the name to her as he nestled his son in his arms.

And it fit. Seth grew up to resemble Abel, both in appearance and temperament.

Eve finally knew contentment, no matter what happened, both in the good and in the sorrow. Like Abel, she resolved to enjoy what God gave to her. How strange that in those early days, when she had had everything, she had still craved more. She had been driven with the desire to leave the garden and explore. Now she wanted nothing more than to stay home and bless her family. The simple joys she had once ignored now became increasingly important. God had made her to be enough in Him, submitted to Him. All the wisdom of the world could not supplant Him. Knowledge without love or restraint brought too high a price.

She continued to tell the first story over and over to her many, many children who came after Seth. In the years that followed, a village spread out in every direction, filled with circular houses and more fields close to the river.

She described how the world was made by God's mighty will. Adam would often join her at the evening fire and share what he remembered with them, their beloved faces bright with awe. She kept the story simple, as did Adam. It never grew larger with the passing years, but it grew weightier, and the urgency to tell the truth never left Eve.

To her older children, she left nothing hidden. Instead, she clarified that despite her failures, it was not too late to find healing. To start over. To seek forgiveness.

One day, a deliverer would come. She would do everything in her power to ensure that the truth endured for as long as it took for Him to arrive. Her lost children might consume themselves with building magnificent cities filled with wondrous sights, but the first story of God's glorious creation and love would endure forever. Those who wanted to learn more of His love and provision would believe and be saved. One day, the deliverer would make everything right again.

And that knowledge gave her great hope.

EPILOGUE

A shining star hovered above Bethlehem, bright enough to rival the moon. An exhausted young mother held her firstborn to her chest and watched him nurse. Her heart felt a peace she could not explain despite the humble surroundings of a manger. Beside her, her husband scooted closer and kissed the top of her head. He placed a large hand on the back of his adopted son, as so many fathers before him had done. He marveled at his child. So tiny, so frail, and yet in this frail form, so much promise waited. The deliverer had finally come.

Meanwhile, in the sloping green fields lined with hilly terrain and a multitude of caves where the sheep took refuge, shepherds dropped their staffs as the sky flashed with zooming lights. Far too many to count. The angels took form, singing as one as they filled the dark void.

"Glory to God in the highest, and peace on earth to people who enjoy His favor!"

The angel raised a gleaming hand, stilling the startled cry of the oldest of the shepherds who remained brave enough to face the sky. The glory of the Lord shone around the shepherds, and they were terrified. But the angel said to them, "Do not be afraid. I bring you good news that will cause great joy for all the people. Today, in the town of David, a Savior has been born to you; he is the Messiah, the Lord. This will be a sign to you: You will find a baby wrapped in cloths and lying in a manger."

And the first woman ever created, who stood beside the glittering Tree of Life in the golden heavenly realm, knelt in worship and rejoiced to see her Father's will fulfilled.

Letter from
THE AUTHOR

Dear Reader,

I was delighted to write the story of Eve, even if I experienced trepidation after signing the contract. After all, Eve takes us back to the very beginning of the world. It's easy to cast judgment on the first woman and ask why she threw it all away for a piece of fruit. However, Eve's sin highlights a serious issue we all wrestle with. Who do we trust to guide us? Do we lean on our feelings and our so-called wisdom? Or do we trust God's Word, regardless of how we feel inside or what we hear from others?

Sadly, we've all sinned and need redemption. Eve is truly a story of firsts. Without a mother, and with an eventual separation from God, her Father, I envisioned a woman trying her very best to reclaim what she lost and eventually realizing that she simply couldn't go back to the life she had once enjoyed. She needed someone to bridge the gap. Someone to rescue her.

Her faith is tested in the death of one son and the banishment of another. Yet God had promised a deliverer. Like Eve, we have the choice of believing God will do what He says He will do, or choosing to doubt Him because of what the world or our current circumstances dictate.

I'd like to think that Eve learned some hard-earned lessons both about the sovereignty and the grace of God. Even when Eve lost both of her sons, God still provided Seth. Of course, Eve and Adam would have to impart their faith and wisdom for Seth to glean the benefits. As I wrote the novel, I pictured a flawed couple very much in love. Despite their brokenness, they fight for their relationship and grow closer in the end.

Eve's story offers so much hope. Even when we make terrible mistakes, God forgives and redeems us if we seek repentance for our sins. He doesn't always take away the consequences of our choices, but we can trust that His ultimate plan will remain in place. He works all things for the good of those who love Him. He searches for the one lost sheep in order to bring it back home. Eve's loss of both sons, the obedient child and the rebellious child, resonates today. One can never discount the prayers of a mother who longs to see her children restored. No one understood this more than Jesus when telling the story of the prodigal son returning to his father at long last.

Regarding the historical sections, I portrayed Adam and Eve as fairly sophisticated, curious, and inventive. The Sumerians, one of the earliest cultures near the Iraq region or the Euphrates River, offer examples of mud-brick homes, first circular in a tent formation, then later built with courtyards, bathrooms, and flat-topped roofs. Perhaps their technology was merely an echo from an earlier time. I hope for Eve's sake that at some point, she could leave a suffocating cave and find a better version of home.

The First Daughter: Eve's Story

Did Adam and Eve eat meat? Possibly not, since God originally offered vegetables and fruit. Later in Genesis, it's clear God encouraged Noah to eat meat after the flood and introduced a fear into the animals when encountering men. Perhaps Adam hunted for additional skins for clothing or household goods. We know from Genesis that Abel took care of the flock, offering the fat as a sacrifice. Why a flock? Sheep provide wool and milk. Also, the fatter the sheep, the greater the wool production. Abel truly gave the very best he had.

In addition, there is some thought that prehistoric man ate eggs, albeit raw. I've used modern terms for vegetables, but we don't know what they looked like during the earliest years. Medieval carrots are described as purple. I hope the reader will forgive my artistic license by creating a one-of-a-kind tree with unusual fruit.

What kind of city did Cain build? We'll never truly know since that version of the world ended with the flood. However, the Gobekli Tepe temple complex in Turkey may offer a picture. Some archeologists view it as the oldest temple or ancient city, predating Sumerian culture. It comprises an underground temple with snake worship and animal motifs. The Gobekli temple also contains stone carved pillars, mud-brick structures, gardens, and animal husbandry. I do not believe the temple in Turkey predates the global flood. However, it is currently rocking the archeology world, challenging long established assumptions regarding ancient cultures.

Ancient man's ingenuity can't be discounted when examining past archeology. Nor his artistic ability, as seen in the prehistoric cave paintings in France. We can see some of the finest examples of art to this day in Chauvet, France, with detailed animal drawings showcasing seasons and constellations. Burials with treasured items, much like the ancient Egyptian customs, indicate an awareness of the afterlife. In addition, should you ever visit the southern Florida area near West Palm Beach, some of the natural history museums offer wonderful examples of Cain's spear sling used for hunting large prey. The *atlatl* can propel a flexible, pointed shaft, which has more in common with a dart than an arrow, at high speeds across long distances. The atlatl acted as a bow or a lever, containing a hook or a spurt at the end to hold the spear, ensuring greater strength and force than if the spear was thrown alone. Paleo-Indian cultures used them along the Florida coast.

The beginnings of culture and ingenuity were taking shape. Man took over the land and subdued it to his will in order to recreate a bit of Eden once again. Adam's sons were farmers, growing produce and discovering animal husbandry. Later, and within Adam's lifetime, Cain's offspring were credited as the fathers of metal working, nomad tent life, and musical instruments. Not only that, Cain constructed a city. Imagine if we could live to reach nine hundred years. What kind of knowledge would we accumulate? What kind of art or music could we produce as we learned to build skill upon skill?

How many children did Eve have and who did those children marry? We don't know the answer to either question. It's more than likely that Eve had plenty of children in between Abel and Seth. However, for the sake of a shorter novel, I described the lives of only five children. If Adam lived over nine hundred years, and his wife a similar length, it is quite possible she had hundreds of children. It is feasible those children married each other, creating additional family lines equally large. It would not take long before the gene pool would widen considerably. While today we abhor sibling marriages, and appropriately so, in Eve's time such a union would have been a probability, and their genetic code was pure enough to allow for such a thing. Even Abraham married his half sister. Egyptian kings of the old and middle dynasties married siblings as well. However, such unions were specifically forbidden in Leviticus 18:6–18 and are to be avoided today.

Finally, Matthew Henry's description of Eve might be one of the most profound and sweetest thoughts when considering the role of men and women, particularly in marriage. "The woman was made of a rib out of the side of Adam; not made out of his head to rule over him, nor out of his feet to be trampled upon by him, but out of his side to be equal with him, under his arm to be protected, and near his heart to be beloved."

Blessings,
Jenelle Hovde

A SCHOLAR'S VIEW OF THE GARDEN OF EDEN

On a hot summer day with the thermometer climbing toward 105 degrees outdoors, one might well lean back under the air conditioner with a glass of iced tea in hand and wonder where the Garden of Eden, that earthly paradise, might be today. When one reads Adam and Eve's story, the same thoughts bubble up. Where was this wonderful place? Could any remnant be left? Might we pull out a world map and find the exact spot just in case we wanted to go there?

Actually, that idea raises one of the most fascinating questions in the Bible. Let's see if we can find some hints about where the Garden of Eden actually existed.

Genesis suggests that the Garden was "eastward in Eden." The scripture describes the Garden as containing one river that diverged and became the source of four other rivers. Pishon ran through a land filled with gold. Gihon watered the entire land of Cush. The other two rivers were the Tigris and the Euphrates. That's the big clue.

The Tigris and Euphrates merge once again and run into the Persian Gulf. Consequently, the Garden could have been located where the rivers come together near the Gulf. Following that theory, a British archaeologist concluded that the Garden was located in Iran near Tabriz, but few agreed with that opinion. Other conjectures became even more extreme. In 1498, Christopher Columbus thought he had found Eden when he discovered the South American mainland. And in the nineteenth century, the earliest leaders of the Mormon church, including Brigham Young, Heber Kimball, and George Cannon, taught their followers that the Garden of Eden had been located in Jackson County, Missouri. They held to the belief that after the expulsion from the Garden, Adam and Eve settled to the northeast in Daviess County, Missouri.

Ezekiel 28:12–19 seems to locate the Garden of Eden in Lebanon. Ezekiel attacks the King of Tyre for having begun well, but then becoming corrupted. He describes the king as being elegantly dressed but now cast out of the Garden to meet a despicable end. Some scholars conclude that the "Garden of the Gods," an old Sumerian analogue for the biblical garden, related to a mountain sanctuary in Lebanon.

Actually, the name has been translated several different ways. Sometimes called the Garden of God, it also has been called the "Terrestrial Paradise." The Aramaic-language root means "fruitful" or "well-watered." This name has special meaning in desert country. All of these ideas raise the question, "What was the Garden like?"

One of the most interesting answers comes from Jewish texts. In both the *Talmud* and the *Kabbalah* there is a description of two different areas encompassed in the name *Garden of Eden*. The lower Garden is a place of lush vegetation and abundant greenery. The second area is called the Higher *Gan Eden*, or

Higher Garden of Eden, and is inhabited by the righteous, both Jews and Gentiles. Adam and Eve would have lived in the lower Garden while the higher realm could not be seen by mortal eyes.

Rabbis who hold this view believe the Garden of Righteousness will return at the end of time. The righteous will walk with God, and He will lead them in a dance. They will be clothed in garments of light and eternal life. Moreover, they can eat of the Tree of Life. The higher Garden has seven compartments. The founder of Rabbinic Judaism in the late 1990s BC, Yochanan Ben Zakkai, and his disciples will be entitled to one of these compartments.

One tradition about the Garden of Righteousness holds that at death, mankind must first journey through the lower Garden in order to climb to the higher Garden. To reach the lower Garden, one must travel to the Cave of Machpelah, where the patriarchs are buried. The cave is the entry into the Garden and is guarded by a cherub with a flaming sword. As the unworthy approach, they are destroyed. Once the righteous get past the gate and into the Garden, they will find a pillar of smoke and fire that reaches into the upper Garden. The worthy must climb up this column to reach the Higher *Gan Eden*. Far from disappearing physically from the earth, the Garden of Eden takes on an eternal significance.

Now, you might wonder what sort of world Adam and Eve finally entered when they left the Garden. Of course, survival became the urgent need of the day, and it would have been a stark struggle indeed. While Christians generally call this "The Fall" of mankind, Jewish rabbis see it as the upward climb toward higher civilization. Either way, Adam and Eve were confronted with a hard task. Genesis 3:23 tells us they were sent out to till the ground from which Adam was taken. What exactly does that description mean? We can discover two possible answers in this verse.

As the first humans, and as God ordered them, Adam and Eve would have been required to learn to raise livestock and plant crops outside Eden, rather than simply gather what they needed. Their son, Abel, was a sheep herder and Cain tilled the soil (Genesis 4:2).

Soon communities would spring up, where people stayed largely in one place and began to build social networks. The Agricultural Revolution, believed to have started in the Fertile Crescent where farming first began, is another reason to locate the Garden of Eden in the Fertile Crescent area. Tribes were now moving into a more settled situation. Farming made storage possible and that provided more security. Cereals such as wheat, einkorn, and barley were among the first crops domesticated. Lentils, chickpeas, peas, and flax soon followed. The first livestock—sheep and cattle—were domesticated from animals that had been hunted earlier. Milk and meat added new strength to the people's diets. Eventually, writing and the creation of art would develop.

However, human strife did not recede, and we continue to struggle today in countless ways.

Fiction Author
JENELLE HOVDE

Jenelle Hovde writes gentle stories of redemption and hope. She lives in Florida with her husband, close to the ocean for quick writing breaks. When she isn't writing, she homeschools three children and manages two spoiled cats. Her other biblical fiction includes *The Dream Weaver's Bride: Asenath's Story* and *A Harvest of Grace: Ruth and Naomi's Story* with Guideposts Fiction.

Nonfiction Author
ROBERT L. WISE, Ph.D.

The Rev. Robert L. Wise, Ph.D., is the author of thirty-five books and numerous articles published in English, Spanish, Dutch, Chinese, Japanese, and German. On the internet he weekly publishes *Miracles Never Cease* and monthly presents live interviews on YouTube with people who have experienced divine interventions.

Read on for a sneak peek of another exciting story in the Extraordinary Women of the Bible series!

THE ONES JESUS LOVED: MARY & MARTHA'S STORY

BY CAROLE TOWRISS

In the fifteenth year of the reign of Tiberius Caesar—when Pontius Pilate was governor of Judea, [and] Herod tetrarch of Galilee...
—Luke 3:1 (NIV)

Jerusalem, Province of Judea
Nisan 10
Four Days before Pesach

Martha's blood ran cold at the distant sound of pounding hoofbeats. Every muscle in her body struggled to flee, to hide from what was coming, but her legs were as cedar.

"Martha!" A sharp voice cut through her fear as a strong hand grabbed her by the arm, pulling her backward toward the western wall of the temple.

Thank Yahweh for Daniel.

She crept backward, closer to the massive stones of the wall towering behind them, trying to leave a safe distance between the broad, stone-paved street and herself. She perched on her toes and searched north along the Roman-built road that ran beside the temple from Herod's Gate in the north to the Water Gate in the south. The deafening, rhythmic noise of trotting horses, banging drums, and armored men swelled.

He must be close.

Sight abruptly caught up with sound. At the head of the procession was Pontius Pilate. Astride a magnificent white warhorse, Judea's newest Roman governor stared ahead, ignoring the people either cheering for him or cowering below him. The sun caromed off the gleaming silver armor covering both man and beast.

Marching behind him, a line of leather-clad soldiers strutted as one into the City of God. Enormous banners emblazoned with *SPQR—Senatus Populusque Romanus*—The Senate and People of Rome—swayed on silver poles.

Martha moved closer to Daniel as three cohorts filed past, their shields, helmets, and swords boasting of Rome's absolute power over Judea.

Drums thumped. Bridles clinked. Leather creaked. Hooves pounded. Every sight and sound was intentionally, strategically designed to instill awe and terror.

The ranks of soldiers seemed endless, but finally the last row passed under the bridge that connected the temple courts to the Upper City. Just past Martha and Daniel, they turned right, marching through a gate in the wall that cocooned the wealthy upper city from the rest of Jerusalem and her struggling inhabitants. That gate was normally shut and locked. No need to allow the poorer residents to gape and gawk at the villa-sized homes of the elite.

Their final destination was the *praetorium*, the once glorious palace of the wicked king Herod. At his death, his territory had been divided among his sons. Archelaus had received the lion's share but had done such a monstrously bad job that Augustus deposed him and replaced him with a Roman ruler. His brother Antipas governed the Galilee, and Philip ruled even farther north, leaving the palace empty most of the year, since the Roman governors preferred to control Judea from the luxurious seaside city of Caesarea Maritima.

Martha flinched as the gate slammed closed. The procession was over.

Until next year.

Only moments ago, she'd been laughing in the city's market south of the temple, chatting with vendors she'd known and bargained with for most of her life, obtaining those last few items needed for the Pesach meal.

Now she sucked in deep breaths until her heart calmed. "Thank you, Daniel."

"Let's go home." He offered a warm smile, erasing any fear that he thought her foolish.

She stepped away from the wall, squared her shoulders, and shook her head. "He's a day late. He was supposed to arrive yesterday. That's why I came on the second day of the week." She grunted. "I'd really hoped to avoid him this year."

Daniel shrugged. "It's his first year to be in Jerusalem for Pesach. Maybe he took longer in Caesarea to make plans."

"They've had the same plans for almost a hundred years." She swallowed the bitterness that soured her tongue. "At least he left his eagles at home this time."

Daniel chuckled. "I don't think even he would be foolish enough to try that again."

Martha had been among the crowd in Jerusalem last summer, the day Pilate had arrived to succeed Valerius Gratus as *praetor* of Judea. Under cover of night, Pilate had arrived at the praetorium and promptly installed imperial banners all around the city, each one bearing the golden eagle and worse, the image of Tiberius Caesar. The Israelites immediately decried the blatant idolatry.

She scoffed. "I still can't believe he did that. And in such a cowardly way. I thought Romans were fearless."

"Fearless, maybe, but not necessarily the smartest ones around. Most are here as either some sort of reward or punishment. Either way, they think it's an easy assignment. They don't plan to stay long and don't bother to learn about the people they intend to rule."

No one was a better example of that than Pilate. An angry mob had sent him scurrying back to Caesarea last summer, without his banners. The priests promptly sent a delegation demanding he remove the pagan images from the holy city. Instead, Pilate threatened them with death. Negotiations lasted six days, until the Jews showed they were willing to die for the holiness of their God and their city.

The images disappeared within days. Whether it was because he feared further violence or was impressed with their sincerity of belief was uncertain.

"Did you get everything?" Daniel gestured to the wide basket on her arm.

"Let's see." She rummaged through her purchases. "I have horseradish, radishes, and chicory for the bitter herbs. Cinnamon. Oh, I haven't bought oil yet. I wanted to get some olive oil flavored with garlic. I don't have time to get the flavor strong enough. It's on our way back to the gate."

They continued on their way up the road next to the temple. It hadn't taken long for the vendors to return to hawking their wares. Strident voices boasted the choicest olive oil, the finest cloth, the tastiest spices. Martha quickly bought the infused oil, along with an *amphora* of honey. Daniel tucked one pottery container in the crook of each arm.

"Do you need this much for Pesach?"

"We never know when guests may arrive in need of food and shelter." She caught his gaze. "Will you and Enoch be joining us?"

He shook his head. "I think *Abba* is planning to join our relatives in Jerusalem again."

"Oh." She tried to hide her disappointment. Since he and his abba had arrived two years ago, they'd not shared one feast meal with anyone in Bethany. They hadn't yet found their place in the village, hadn't helped with much of anything. That would all change next year, surely. Daniel would be her husband by then.

Daniel led them back under the arched gate north of the temple, leaving the paved streets of the city for the wide, well-traveled dirt path that led to Bethphage and Bethany.

Tension melted away from her shoulders, her neck. The air was sweeter, and away from the crowds, even cooler.

A slight breeze stirred the flowers that emblazoned the hillside, making the climb up the Mount of Olives more enjoyable. Red chamomile and blue alkanet peeked from among fig and olive trees. Olives just beginning to bud emitted a slight musky scent. A crested hoopoe called for its mate. *Oop-oop-oop.*

Jerusalem fell away behind them. Isaiah had called Jerusalem Mount Zion, the place of the Name of the Lord Almighty. But he'd also prophesied Jerusalem would be utterly destroyed because of her faithlessness. Today, knowing both Herod Antipas and Caiaphas, the high priest, would be at the prefect's house tonight currying favor, she believed it wouldn't be long.

Bethany
Eastern slope of the Mount of Olives

Mary cringed. A knife-edged rock pierced the sole of her bare foot as she crouched against the stone wall that surrounded the courtyard of Gershom's home. She ignored the pain and held her breath, trying to remain silent.

Though she couldn't see over the wall, Mary knew precisely what was happening at this moment in the *bet sefer*. Gershom was the *rabbi* of this house of the book, where children studied and memorized the scriptures. He would be sitting on a low stool under the ancient olive tree that dominated the open space, one of the sacred scrolls held gently and reverently in his hands. Nine boys—unless one was ill—would be in a semicircle at the feet of the old man, each with a wax tablet and stylus in his lap, waiting to hear the holy words like a nest of hungry baby birds with their mouths open.

At least that's what they would do if they realized the unfathomable treasure that could be theirs should they but listen. Every walled city in Judea had a teacher, but very few villages the size of Bethany had one. Yet half the boys seemed irritated that they were required to attend school from age five to thirteen.

While she, who would give anything for the privilege, was forbidden. The priest before Gershom had allowed her to study, as did many others teachers in Judea. But Gershom had expelled her, though she could have studied another year.

She reached above her head to grip the edge of the low wall, her fingers just over the top, then pulled herself up slowly, hoping to catch a mere glimpse of the scrolls.

"Today we begin our study of Hallel."

A low groan reached her ears. Probably from Tobiah. He was nearly thirteen, and if it were up to her he would have been banished long ago. He cared nothing for the words of Adonai, and his constant complaints ate at her patience.

"Tobiah, can you tell me what *Hallel* is?" Gershom's voice revealed no irritation with the boy at all. How could he not be frustrated with a student who clearly didn't want to learn?

"I don't know. A *mizmor* of David?"

Mary scoffed. Hallel was *six* psalms, not one, and none of them were written by David.

"Perhaps you should use your voice only when you know the answer," Gershom said.

She suppressed a giggle at the gentle, yet surprising, rebuke.

"Nekoda, can you tell us?"

"Hallel is a prayer. It is made of six *mizmorim*." The boy answered confidently. He was a good student, though one of the youngest.

"And when do we say this prayer?" asked the teacher.

"It is sung for Pesach, *Shavuot*, and *Sukkot*," said Nekoda,

"And *Rosh Hashanah*," added Tobiah.

"No," Gershom corrected Tobiah. "Hallel is not sung at Rosh Hashanah nor at *Yom Kippur*. Who knows why?"

Silence.

For once, Mary did not know the answer either, though she'd often wondered why the songs of praise were not sung on the Day of Atonement.

"We do not sing it at those times because Adonai is then sitting on His throne with the Books of Life and Death open before Him. It is a time for repentance and forgiveness, not a time for joy."

Ah. That made sense.

"But we do sing it at the Feast of *Hanukkah*!" The voice was so soft Mary almost couldn't hear him. Mishael was the youngest, and he loved the holy texts as much as she did.

"Yes. *Toda*, Nekoda and Mishael. Now, who can tell me the first words of each of these mizmorim?"

Mary longed to shout out the answer: *Hallelu yah*. A holy command to praise the Lord. She ached to be part of this group openly studying and rejoicing over the holy words of Adonai instead of hiding behind rough stone and straining to hear.

"Hallelu yah." Mary didn't recognize the voice. Gershom must have a new student. Who could it be? She quickly ran through each family in the village, trying to remember their sons.

"Yes, *todah*, Seth."

Ah yes. Seth, Tobiah's younger brother. Hopefully he wouldn't catch Tobiah's terrible attitude.

"Everyone, repeat after me." Gershom's voice was clear and strong. "Hallelu yah! Servants of Adonai, give praise! Blessed be the name of Adonai from this moment on and forever!"

The boys mumbled the first sentences of the first mizmor of Hallel, words tumbling from their mouths like pebbles.

The prayer threatened to burst from her chest. If she were sitting with the boys, they would hear her in Jerusalem.

"This is not how you praise the Creator of the universe!" Gershom scolded his students. "If you cannot give Him the praise He deserves, He will cause rocks to do it for you! Now, give Him praise! Together!"

The boys recited loudly, though not quite in unison.

"Give praise to the name of Adonai!" Not waiting for the boys, Mary recited the verse silently along with the teacher. "From sunrise until sunset Adonai's name is to be praised. Adonai is high above all nations, His glory above the heavens."

If she could not shout the words aloud along with the boys of Bethany, she would have to settle for allowing her heart to speak.

"Who is like Adonai our God, seated in the heights, humbling Himself to look on heaven and on earth?"

Mary tried to envision Adonai seated on an enormous throne, resplendent in gold and jewels and incomprehensible light, even more magnificent than the temple on the other side of the mount. But such a holy God was beyond her ability to imagine.

"Seth, return to the lesson, please." Gershom's voice was sharp. "We do not wander as we study the holy words."

A short, skinny arm jutted out above her head, followed by a head covered with curly hair. "But Rabbi! There's a girl here!" The newest student peered down at her, a mischievous grin on his dirty face.

Why was he worrying about her instead of studying the sacred scroll held by the rabbi? He was wasting a precious opportunity.

But there was no time to think about that now. Rustling tunics, legs unfolding, and the sound of footsteps on dirt heading her way told her she had been caught.

Mary jumped to her feet and raced down Bethany's only road. The house of the rabbi perched at the northern edge of the village, and her home was at the other end. Still, it was a tiny village, and she'd learned to run—fast.